AIR OF SALVATION

AIR
OF SALVATION

THE STORY OF CHRISTIAN BROADCASTING

Mark Ward, Sr.

Foreword by E. Brandt Gustavson

Baker Books

A Division of Baker Book House Co
Grand Rapids, Michigan 49516

Published by Baker Books
a division of Baker Book House Company
P.O. Box 6287, Grand Rapids, MI 49516-6287

Printed in the United States of America

Library of Congress Cataloging-in-Publication Data

Ward, Mark, 1958–
    Air of salvation : the story of Christian broadcasting / Mark Ward, Sr. ;
foreword by E. Brandt Gustavson.
        p.   cm.
    Includes bibliographical references and index.
    ISBN 0-8010-9732-0
    1. Religious broadcasting—United States—History. 2. Religious
broadcasting—Christianity—History. I. Title.
BV655.2.U6W37   1994
269'.26'0973—dc20
                                             94-17581

Scripture quotations are from the King James Version of the Bible.

To my wife, **Donna,**
a faithful "keeper at home"
and partner in ministry;
and to **Mark** and **Laura,** that
they might be "as arrows are
in the hand of a mighty man."

CONTENTS

Contents

FOREWORD

For seventy-three years the gospel has been broadcast over the airwaves. From its humble beginnings on radio in 1921, to its debut on television in 1940, the Christian message has continued. With hard work behind the scenes, keeping the airwaves open for the gospel has been the goal since the early pioneers and was the primary purpose for founding National Religious Broadcasters (NRB) in 1944.

In this volume, you will see how God has worked through people. You will see the ups and downs of religious broadcasting and gain insight into the forces driving those whose calling was—and is—to preach the gospel.

I'm very appreciative of Mark Ward, who is on the staff of NRB as editor of the *Directory of Religious Media*. We have found him not only to be an outstanding editor, but a skillful author willing to take on the challenge of writing *Air of Salvation*.

As you read this book, let your heart be lifted in praise to our Lord, whose purpose it is to reach men and women, boys and girls, for his glorious kingdom. Christian radio and television, along with all the new media technology, will have many more opportunities to proclaim the gospel message until Jesus comes.

E. Brandt Gustavson, President
National Religious Broadcasters

PREFACE

A ny book assumes a life of its own, often ending up far different than at first intended. So it is with *Air of Salvation*. The project began as National Religious Broadcasters looked ahead to 1994 and the fiftieth anniversary of its founding. Such a milestone could not pass without providing a record. But it was soon clear that a history of NRB could only be understood in the context of overall developments in Christian broadcasting. Thus was our vision enlarged. We started simply to recount the history of an organization and ended up writing the colorful story of a great industry that has been greatly used of God.

With such a vision, the right approach was easy to decide. *Air of Salvation* would not be a dry historical record but would read like a story—with all the excitement, the personalities, and the often incredible events that have made gospel broadcasting what it is today. To our knowledge, *Air of Salvation* is the only volume that weaves these stories into one chronological narrative of the industry, as each individual story illustrates the larger story of how and why religious broadcasting has developed over the years.

Our purpose in writing this book is threefold: first, NRB hopes you will be blessed and inspired, that you will put down this volume and say, "God has been at work in Christian broadcasting!" Second, we desire that Christian broadcasters who read *Air of Salvation* will learn from the past, that they might avoid its mistakes, and apply its lessons as a guide to using the new media technologies of the future. And third, because gospel radio and television enjoy general freedom today, it is easy to assume this has always been so—and always will be. Yet most Christians today are unaware that gospel programs were once banned, that freedom to use the airwaves was only won with great difficulty, and that assaults on this freedom continue today. For every believer who reads *Air of Salvation*, we trust that there will be a new appreciation of what it takes to put Christian programming on the air.

One of the joys in publishing *Air of Salvation* is that the blessings I have gained in writing the book can now be passed on to you. I was often amazed how, like ripples in a pond, the work of one broadcaster would affect so many across the decades. Jerry Falwell came to Christ by the ministry of Charles Fuller, who in turn was saved under the preaching of Paul Rader. Billy Graham, Trans World Radio, Youth for Christ, the Christian Broadcasting Network, and the New Inspirational Network can all be traced back to Percy Crawford (who was saved at the same church as Charles Fuller). And because one woman faithfully prayed twelve years for a wayward husband, Paul Myers and *Haven of Rest* gave rise to the global ministries of World Vision and the Far East Broadcasting Company.

I hope you get as much from reading *Air of Salvation* as I did from writing it. When I was finished, I put the book down and said, "God has been at work in Christian broadcasting!"

Prologue

THE MOMENT OF TRUTH

1944

William Ward Ayer found it hard to believe. Hard to believe that only twenty years ago he had listened to a radio broadcast for the very first time. Hard to believe that twenty years later he was preaching by radio each week to a quarter of a million people throughout the largest city in America. And hard to believe it would all be gone, suddenly, along with all the other radio gospel preachers, driven off the air not by lack of funds or listeners but by men who professed to name the name of Christ.

As he thought the matter over, Ayer could remember the day in 1922 when he first heard the crackle and whine of a neighbor's old crystal radio set. Even after twenty years, the memory was still fresh. Back then he was a dark-haired young preacher with a ready smile and a set of dark, penetrating eyes. He had recently accepted the call to a small Baptist church in Valparaiso, Indiana, only fifty miles southeast of Chicago. Compared to Mason City and Atlanta, towns in downstate Illinois where Ayer had pastored his first two churches, Valparaiso was a big place. With so many people to meet, Ayer was always busy knocking on doors, talking with folks about the gospel and inviting them down to church.

It was while he was out visiting that he came across a neighbor who had just built one of those new crystal radio sets. Ayer was curious, and when the man invited him inside to listen, he gladly agreed. Though he had never heard a broadcast before, he had heard a lot about radio. The nation's first regular broadcast station had begun operation in Pittsburgh only a year or so earlier. Since then, stations had begun springing up all over the country. Everybody was talking about radio! Now as he went with his neighbor to the back room of the house, Ayer could listen for himself. He found a place to sit down, put a set of earphones on, and carefully adjusted the delicate crystal receiver. After the squeals and screeches died away, he could hear a voice and some music coming from Chicago—more than fifty miles away!

That was in 1922. Back then, Ayer had to admit, he had no idea how radio would revolutionize society and the worldwide propagation of the gospel. His own introduction to the gospel had come in 1916, when he "walked the sawdust trail" at a Billy Sunday revival meeting in Boston. He was a restless young man from New Brunswick, Canada, twenty-four years old, and had run away from home at age five when his mother died. But when "The Baseball Evangelist" preached about redemption in Christ, Ayer knew that his search was over. Soon afterward he enrolled at Chicago's Moody Bible Institute, and when he graduated in 1919, the memory of Dwight L. Moody's great crusades was still the model for evangelizing the masses.

Now in 1942, just twenty years after hearing that old crystal radio set, Ayer could reach more people in one day than Moody or Sunday could reach in a year! So much had changed, both in his own life and in the ministry of the gospel. After fourteen years as a pastor in Indiana and Ontario, he had been called to New York City's famous Calvary Baptist Church. His sermons were aired each week on radio station WHN, beamed by fifty thousand watts of power to a potential audience of twenty-two million! Not only had hundreds of people come to Christ through the radio outreach, but the broadcasts had strengthened the ministry of the church. Attendance at Calvary Baptist had risen from four hundred to more than sixteen hundred people. More than five thousand persons had walked the aisle to receive Jesus Christ as their Savior. And the church was publishing a widely read periodical, *The Calvary Pulpit*, that expanded the ministry to thousands more each month.

Like the Turn of a Dial

Ayer was not alone. Pioneer broadcasters such as Paul Rader and Donald Grey Barnhouse had begun preaching coast to coast a decade ago. National network programs such as *The Lutheran Hour* with Walter A. Maier and the *Old-Fashioned Revival Hour* with Charles E. Fuller had built audiences in the millions. By 1942, Maier was receiving more mail than *Amos 'n' Andy*, and Fuller was the biggest name on the Mutual Broadcasting Network, spending nearly thirty thousand dollars a week and purchasing 50 percent more airtime than the next largest secular broadcaster. Altogether, the Mutual network received more than one-fourth of its revenues from religious broadcasters.

Then suddenly, like the turn of a radio dial, Ayer was faced with being taken off the air. Fuller, Maier, Barnhouse, Rader, and all the other radio gospel preachers across America would also be gone. What had happened? The more Ayer thought about it, the less he could believe it. Gospel programs were undeniably giving great spiritual benefit and comfort to millions of Americans. It seemed that the country, now engaged in the terrible struggle of World War II, was enjoying a religious reawakening. Listeners across the country were supporting the broadcasts with their contributions while continuing to give to their local churches. Never before were so many Americans being reached with the gospel of Christ.

Who then wanted these programs off the air? Commercial broadcasters who wanted the airtime for themselves? Radio advertisers who favored more popular programming? No, the threat came from within the church itself! Ayer had heard these critics before, people who said religion was "too sacred" to be bought and sold on the radio like tooth powder or laundry soap. They claimed independent preachers were not accountable to anyone and could not be trusted with the public airwaves. And in 1942 they acted, led by the Federal (later National) Council of Churches. A new set of network regulations had been proposed. Religious programming would only be aired as a public service during free or "sustaining" time donated by the networks. Slots would be allocated to "responsible" religious broadcasters, approved by local and national church councils that "represented" the Protestant community. Independent preachers like Ayer, Fuller, and Maier would be left out.

There won't be a single evangelical, biblical broadcast of the gospel on the air in America if something isn't done immediately, Ayer thought to himself. To alert his friends and listeners, he rushed into print with a lengthy article, "Will Americans Be Allowed to Broadcast the Gospel?" in *The Calvary Pulpit*. Response was encouraging, but without an organized effort it wouldn't be enough. The Federal Council of Churches represented less than 40 percent of Protestantism, but it was the only group speaking for the historic Protestant church movement. When the Council spoke, the New York network executives listened.

Meet Me in St. Louis

Ayer, however, was not the only preacher worried about the freedom to broadcast the gospel. Other men of God from around the country had seen the need to organize. When a group of leading evangelical pastors and ministers wanted to organize a national conference, Ayer invited the planning committee to meet in the offices of Calvary Baptist Church. By meeting in New York City, the committee could stay abreast of developments at the radio networks and the Federal Council of Churches that might affect their agenda. The planning required months of work, but at last a general conference was convened in April 1942 in St. Louis. More than 150 evangelical leaders from scores of groups and denominations arrived from every part of America.

Among those present was Harold John Ockenga, pastor of the famous Park Street Church in Boston. Recently, after corresponding with leading gospel broadcasters, he had met with executives of the National Broadcasting Company (NBC) at its Boston affiliate, WBZ. He sadly reported, "We shall have absolutely no opportunity of sharing equally in the broadcast facilities of that great network" unless the evangelical movement could organize on a national basis. "We are a very large minority, perhaps a majority, in America," he declared, "which is discriminated against because of the folly of our divided condition." Ockenga explained that NBC recognized three faith groups—Catholic, Protestant, and Jewish—and divided sustaining (free) time religious programs between them. The network considered the Federal Council of Churches to be the sole representative of Protestantism and would not sell airtime to religious broadcasters. Pastors and ministers not approved by the Federal Council were simply not aired on NBC. A similar policy was enforced at the Columbia Broadcasting System (CBS). And though Mutual, the third major network, sold time to Charles Fuller and others, executives there were wavering.

To keep gospel radio on the air, Ockenga said, "This millstone of rugged independency which has held back innumerable movements before, in which individual leaders must be the whole hog or none, must be utterly repudiated by every one of us." As those words sank in, Ayer felt he too must speak out. He was among the most prominent and respected of the fundamentalist evangelical leaders, and his voice would be needed to help bring the movement together. Ayer approached the lectern, cleared his throat, and then declared to the assembled conference, "Millions of evangelical Christians, if they had a common voice and a common meeting place, would exercise under God an influence that would save American democracy."

From then on, things began to happen. The conference moved to establish a National Association of Evangelicals for United Action, electing Ockenga as temporary president and appointing Ayer to serve on the executive committee. By August a twice-monthly newspaper, *United Evangelical Action*, was rolling off the presses. Delegates called for a constitutional convention the following spring—and when that meeting took place in May 1943, more than a thousand evangelical representatives were in attendance. Within four months the newly formed NAE opened an office in Washington to represent the interests of evangelicals in matters ranging from religious liberty to military chaplains. Discussions began on cooperative ventures in missions, world relief, and many other areas.

The Networks Pull the Plug

But the issue that first galvanized the evangelical community seemed as far away from victory as ever. Ayer was stunned, along with every other gospel broadcaster in America, when in late 1943 the Mutual network announced it would place nearly impossible restrictions on the sale of airtime for religious programs. Now the evangelical community was cut off from all three major radio networks. And what if local affiliate stations, such as Ayer's own WHN, followed their example? The voices opposed to paid religious programs were becoming louder and more insistent, and they had won over the networks by playing on fears of questionable on-air fund-raising in the name of religion and the specter of different faiths attacking each other over the airwaves.

These issues involved ethics. Ayer had to admit that, while the great majority of evangelical radio preachers were godly, honest men—it was public record, for example, that the *Old-Fashioned Revival Hour* spent 94.5 percent of donated funds for purchasing airtime and only 5.5 percent for overhead—there were some unscrupulous profiteers taking money in the name of God. To reverse the networks' ban on paid religious programs, gospel broadcasters must show they could police themselves and voluntarily enforce a strong code of ethics. That would require a concentrated national effort. But the National Association of Evangelicals, though less than a year old, was already busy in many different and important directions. The group was promoting evangelical applicants for the military chaplaincy, helping ministerial and missionary candidates obtain draft deferments, assisting mission boards with wartime travel restrictions, coordinating church relief efforts, monitoring federal legislation, and much more. Could any of these vital projects be sacrificed? Could the NAE do all these things and effectively police broadcasters too?

Down to Business

The stakes were high. "If religious radio is relegated to sustaining (free) time only," Ayer argued to anyone who would listen, "it will be reduced to the minimum and spread over such a wide variety of religious ideas as to spoil its effectiveness." The 1943 NAE constitutional convention in Chicago had appointed a committee on religious broadcasting. And J. Elwin Wright, the NAE executive secretary, had spoken out forcefully to industry groups and government officials. But it was time for broadcasters to take the lead in their own fight. Under the auspices of the broadcasting committee, a special session was slated for the second annual NAE convention in Columbus, Ohio. Some 150 radio preachers were invited to the April 1944 meeting to gauge interest in forming a national association of religious broadcasters.

When Ayer arrived in Columbus, he could see the group was ready for business. In the room were nearly one hundred of the nation's top evangelical broadcasters. Those present included Charles Fuller of the *Old-Fashioned Revival Hour*; Eugene Bertermann, business manager for *The Lutheran Hour*; Martin DeHaan of *The Radio Bible Class*; Thomas Zimmerman of the Assemblies of God denomination; Torrey Johnson, a religious broadcaster and later the founder of Youth for Christ; John Zoller of *Christ for Everyone*; James DeForest Murch of *The Christians' Hour*; Bob Jones, Sr., founder of Bob Jones University; Paul Myers of *Haven of Rest*; Dale Crowley, Sr., of *Right Start for the Day*; Charles Leaming of the *Faith Gospel Broadcast*; Myron Boyd of *Light and Life Hour*; and Glenn Tingley of *Radio Revival*.

As a member of the NAE executive committee, Ayer was a logical choice to assume temporary chairmanship of the conference. In starting the meeting, he set an urgent tone. Sports, politics, and news had unlimited freedom, he pointed out, while religious broadcasting was continually being put under restriction. "We must maintain our freedom of speech in America," Ayer believed, "whether it be in the pulpit or on the street corner or over the radio." One by one, each man spoke about his concerns for the future of gospel radio. Zimmerman pointed out how the networks were limiting the scope of Christian broadcasts by their sustaining time policies. Tingley suggested modernist churches were worried about radio preachers taking money from their congregations and that was why they wanted to keep all religious broadcasts off the air except their own. Johnson warned their opponents had strong political leverage and that religious broadcasters "must put our own house in order and ensure that none of us would conduct ourselves in the ministry in anything less than the highest ethical ideals."

The Motion Carries

The discussion went back and forth as the delegates voiced their opinions. Then a quiet Baptist minister from Muscatine, Iowa, asked to be recognized. Until then he had not spoken much, but now Vincent Brushwyler had something to say. "I move that we form a national association of gospel broadcasters, to be affiliated with the National Association of Evangelicals." A second to the motion was quickly heard and the question was approved by unanimous vote. There were details to be decided, and as James DeForest Murch later recalled, "The exact place of [the new group] in relationship to the NAE was to be worked out in later conventions." But in that moment on April 12, 1944, what has been known since that day as National Religious Broadcasters was born.

The delegates then quickly got down to business. Ayer was confirmed as president and charged with drafting a code of ethics that would form the basis of evangelical response to the threat against religious broadcasting. Dale Crowley was elected secretary, and at his suggestion the name National Religious Broadcasters was chosen. Murch was asked to draft a constitution and bylaws, which would be presented at a convention to be held at Chicago in September 1944. And before adjourning, the delegates adopted a statement of faith, accepting the Bible as the inspired Word of God.

When he returned home to New York, Ayer had much work to do. He had committees to organize, meetings to schedule, people to see, letters to write. And he was still pastor of Calvary Baptist Church with its many outreaches and programs. But before turning to the work at hand, Ayer thought once more about Valparaiso, Indiana, and the day he heard that old crystal radio set. Hard to believe that in a single generation radio had shown the way to reach the whole world with the Good News of salvation in Christ.

However, the opposition was strong—and was winning. Even now, religious programs around the country were being canceled. Yet when the moment of truth had come, the defenders of the gospel were ready to join the battle.

1

THE EARLY PIONEERS

1921–1927

Rev. Lewis B. Whittemore was just a little bit nervous. It was only a normal Sunday vespers service, he told himself, even if it was the first Sunday of the New Year 1921. Of course, it was somewhat unusual for a junior associate to take the pulpit on such a significant date, especially at Calvary Episcopal Church. It ranked among the best known institutions in Pittsburgh, and the soaring Gothic Revival steeple was a city landmark. Yet the senior pastor had confidence in him, and Whittemore wanted to prove that trust was not misplaced.

Nevertheless, he admitted his own presence in the pulpit was not the only unusual thing about this service. At seminary they had not prepared him for the two radio engineers, one Catholic and the other Jewish, who were setting up some odd-looking equipment in the front of the chapel. But the service must be as normal as possible—those were the senior pastor's instructions—so Whittemore dressed them in choir robes and hoped for the best. If they could only stay quiet, and those machines of theirs did not make too much noise, maybe everything would be all right.

From the look of the wires and tubes, not to mention the big, ungainly microphone on the pulpit, Whittemore admitted the senior pastor might be right. Maybe radio was just a passing fad. And anyway, how could the hookup work when the radio station was nearly ten miles from the church? He couldn't blame the pastor for taking the night off, especially after the busy Christmas season. This radio business was all a bunch of advertising hype. The management at KDKA just wanted another marketing triumph by broadcasting the "first" radio church service.

The First Religious Broadcaster

Whittemore remembered when the matter first came up. It started, like a lot of other troubles, with the church choir. One of the men was an engineer for Westinghouse, the company that owned KDKA. The station had been in regular operation for only two months. But what a start! When KDKA came on the air to broadcast returns of the Harding-Cox presidential election, fewer than a thousand radio operators across the country could pick it up. The program itself originated from a hastily rigged, makeshift studio. But the broadcast created a national sensation, almost as much as the election itself. Newspaper editorials were calling it the beginning of a new era.

However, KDKA had competition. Most observers gave the station credit for being the first to offer regularly scheduled broadcasts. But that didn't stop WWJ of Detroit from claiming it started more than two months earlier. And WBZ of Springfield (later Boston), Massachusetts, was aiming by September to be the first station licensed for regular broadcasting by the Department of

Commerce. The University of Wisconsin also claimed the nation's "first" broadcast station, since its operation had grown from an experimental station established in 1915, a year before the predecessor of KDKA began tested transmissions.

So KDKA was in a race, and scoring "firsts" was part of the Westinghouse marketing plan. The giant electrical company, aware that most radio sets then in use were amateur jobs built at home, wanted to drum up demand for its ready-made models. Regular broadcasts over KDKA were the basis of its strategy, and creating public excitement about new programs was the key to finding an audience. Whittemore had already heard the announcements, urging listeners to start the New Year on January 2 with the inspiration of a Sunday vespers service. They made it sound like a big event. But of course, he was under orders to handle things just like a normal evening service.

And that's what Whittemore did. Once the music started and he could concentrate his attention on the service, the big microphone on the pulpit and the two engineers in choir robes weren't so bad. Even the radio equipment was quiet enough. The congregation did not seem to mind but took everything in stride. When it was over, KDKA said the hookup worked fine. Later the station said response was so favorable they wanted to make Calvary Episcopal a regular Sunday night feature. Imagine that! Of course, Whittemore knew he was just filling in. He wasn't surprised to learn the senior pastor would be resuming the pulpit in the future. After all, Sunday services should be kept as normal as possible.

Direct from City Hall

With the broadcast of the 1920 presidential election, a smart politician could see that radio had possibilities. And Mayor William Hale Thompson of Chicago was a smart politician. The Great War was behind, the Machine Age ahead, and the voters of 1922 wanted virtue *and* progress. The mayor knew how to give it to them.

First, Mayor Thompson would give them a new radio station. The people were already talking about it! The first broadcast was set for June 17, from the roof of city hall, with a dedication in his honor. The new station was even being named WHT, the mayor's own initials. Now he had to arrange a program that would give the occasion a proper solemnity. Maybe something religious?

The mayor thought a moment, then recalled a preacher in town who had a knack for getting people excited. His church was one of the biggest in the city. He was president of an international religious organization. And like Chicago's own Dwight L. Moody, he traveled across America speaking in great outdoor crusades to thousands of people. Suppose the mayor of Chicago invited him to preach a nationwide service by radio, direct from city hall? Now that would be progress! And it certainly would not hurt for the mayor's name to be mentioned alongside a man of the church. Virtue *and* progress. An unbeatable combination!

As for the preacher, Paul Rader was glad enough to accept the mayor's invitation. He would do anything, take any opportunity, to reach people with the gospel of Christ. Last year, on November 27, the *Radio Church of America* had debuted from New York as the first continuous religious program on the airwaves. Since then, a few others had followed. Even some churches were looking into radio. Six months ago, on December 22, the Church of the Covenant (now National Presbyterian Church) in Washington, D.C., had become the first religious organization to obtain a broadcast license. But inwardly, Rader was inclined to be only cautiously optimistic. "Tabernaclism" was the best way, he firmly believed, to evangelize large numbers of people. He had seen the power of preaching, in person, to the masses. Could wires and microphones and a scratchy voice from a homemade radio ever match the fire and energy of such preaching? Could the working of the Holy Spirit, so vital in bringing an audience under conviction, be transmitted over the airwaves? Rader had his doubts.

Without that "Old Time Power," as Rader liked to say, he could preach for a month of Sundays and never win a single convert. He knew. It had taken all the power of the Holy Spirit to turn his own life back to God. Rader remembered those days, hardly a decade ago, when he was disillusioned with the ministry and vowed never to return. The son of a Methodist pastor and revivalist from Denver, he had been to three universities. When he moved east in 1906 to pastor an elite Congregational church in Boston, Rader felt proud and honored. He was only twenty-seven years old and had never even attended seminary.

Before long, however, he was moved again—to Oregon. After two churches in two years, Rader began to wonder about his vocation. He was a rugged individualist, a former prospector, prizefighter, broncobuster, and football player. And he looked like it, a spark plug of a man with a round, pugnacious face. He was not yet thirty, and already his minister's robes were getting too tight. What was the use? That year, 1908, he resigned his pastorate and moved to New York. Maybe here, he told himself, a man who liked action could find it.

His Whole Heart

For the next three years Rader drifted, fighting the Lord and going his own way. Organized religion was dull and confining— certainly not for a man like Paul Rader. Then he heard about a new Christian movement, based in New York, one that disdained hierarchy and emphasized an active faith. The more Rader heard about the Christian and Missionary Alliance, the more he came under the "Old Time Power" of the Holy Spirit. It was a battle! Rader was a restless young man, dissatisfied with the ministry, yet God had other plans. At last in 1911, Rader gave up the fight and surrendered his life to serve the Lord.

Soon he was out on the street corners of New York, moved by the Spirit of God to proclaim Christ to all who would listen. Now that he had given the Lord his whole heart, God began to use the young preacher. Within a year Rader rejoined the ministry as an associate at Pittsburgh's Christian and Missionary Alliance Tabernacle, and in 1915 he was called to pastor the famous Moody Church in Chicago. Seven years later he felt led of God to begin a new church, Chicago Gospel Tabernacle, that quickly became one of the largest congregations in the city. Throughout his days in Chicago, Rader was in great demand as a revival speaker. In cities and towns across America, he preached in temporary "tabernacles" seating audiences from three hundred to three thousand and saw scores of people come to salvation in Christ.

When CMA founder A. B. Simpson went home to the Lord in 1919, Rader was chosen to lead the growing movement as international president. He urged the group to organize regional units for supporting nondenominational "tabernaclism," and envisioned great evangelistic campaigns that might continue daily for months at a time.

Between his ambitious agenda, his pastorate, his speaking tours, and his frequent trips to New York as CMA president, Rader had time for little else. So when the mayor of Chicago invited him to preach by radio from city hall, Rader was grateful but did not expect too much. After all, even the word *radio* had only been coined a decade ago, when the U.S. Navy decided the term *wireless* was too broad. Just one sermon and that would be it. He had so many other things to do.

Old Time Power

When Rader arrived at city hall bringing with him a brass quartet, the group was quickly ushered to the roof of the building. There in the open air, the men were led to a small booth slapped together with unfinished Peg-Boards. It looked like a sentry box, with a hole cut in one of the sides. "You just get ready and point your instruments at the hole there in the side of the box," a technician told the puzzled musicians, "and when I say play, you play." The clock ticked off the seconds until the broadcast, and then a voice shouted, "Play!" Suddenly, an old telephone receiver was shoved through the opening. The quartet struck up a lively chorus. Rader stepped up to the "microphone." He thought it strange, speaking to an invisible audience in a makeshift studio that was empty except for a few staff and engineers. But as he warmed to his message, the "Old Time Power" took hold and Rader preached fervently about the need of every person to find eternal salvation in Jesus Christ. When it was over, there were no shouts of amen, no altar calls, no lines of men and women coming down the aisles to trust Christ as Savior. Rader simply stepped back from the telephone receiver and stopped speaking. That was the end of it.

Within days, however, public response surpassed anything Rader expected. Letters and telegrams and reports of the working of God began pouring into the offices of the Chicago Gospel Tabernacle. Rader was flabbergasted. But characteristically, he was soon ready to act. One of the young musicians on that first broadcast, Clarence Jones, never forgot how the fiery preacher showed "a ready comprehension and acceptance of radio as a means of getting the gospel to the unchurched masses. . . . [He] perceived that here was a twentieth-century miracle method to preach the first-century message to a wider audience than could ever crowd the biggest tabernacle, so he went all out for radio."

Rader began seeking opportunities to broadcast the gospel over other Chicago radio stations. He heard about a station that was idle on Sundays, and arranged to use its transmitter that day for fourteen hours of programs. The operation became a once-a-week station, WJBT or "Where Jesus Blesses Thousands." Sunday evening services at Chicago Gospel Tabernacle were aired each week, and soon capacity crowds of five thousand people flocked to the church to see the preacher whose radio messages had thrilled them. After the service Rader stayed around to broadcast two popular evening programs, *March of the Ages* and *The Back Home Hour.* "Well, fellows, tonight it's going to be the fall of Jericho," was all the idea he would give his staff, as the men scrambled for hymns and songs that fit the theme and narration for the night.

In 1924, Rader stepped down as president of the Christian and Missionary Alliance, then left the group a year later to organize a new worldwide missions enterprise, Christian World Couriers. Through it all, the broadcasts continued stronger than ever. As radio networks began to emerge, Rader was among the first to purchase airtime and build a nationwide audience for the gospel. By 1930 his program, *The Breakfast Brigade,* was heard each morning on CBS. Yet despite his drive for careful human planning and preparation, the "Old Time Power" always came first. "He showed us by example," said Jones, "to depend entirely upon the Holy Spirit for the unction of heaven upon the Word."

Unction Can Be Transmitted

Not far from Chicago, another young Christian and Missionary Alliance pastor listened with interest to the radio ministry of Paul Rader. Of course, he told himself, Omaha was nothing like the great Windy City to the east. Nothing around but prairie for miles and miles. He knew that when Rader, then CMA president, sent him to Nebraska as superintendent of the church's western district. And as far as Rev. R. R. Brown of the Omaha Gospel Tabernacle was concerned, the notion of a radio outreach never crossed his mind.

Nevertheless, when the folks at WOAW (later WOW) approached him, Brown thought it was an interesting idea. The new Omaha radio station had just opened on Monday. They wanted him to bring a message on their first Sunday of operation—April 8, 1923—then be the station's regular minister. Well, it was an honor, especially since he'd been in town less than a year. And even if just about every pastor in Omaha had turned it down before they got around to asking him! Besides, it was a chance to preach the gospel. And it *would* be interesting to see how radio really worked. So he agreed to come that first Sunday but decided to wait and see before accepting the offer to be a regular speaker.

When that Sunday came, Brown went down early to the radio station. They showed him how to approach the microphone, where to stand, how to speak. It was certainly very interesting, even if he wasn't so sure it would really work like they said. They claimed his voice might be heard for hundreds of miles. How could that be? But he delivered his sermon anyway—though giving the gospel to a hunk of wire and metal was a lot different than any kind of preaching he ever knew.

After his message was done, Brown was ready to go home and rest up for Sunday services. He had had his chance to see what radio was like. His curiosity was satisfied. He was glad to say he had done it at least this once. But on the way out, a man was waiting for him at the station door. He was red-faced and excited, huffing and puffing and completely out of breath. Then, as he gasped out his story between breaths, it was Brown's turn to be excited. The man had heard the broadcast, had come under the conviction of the Holy Spirit and trusted Jesus Christ as his Savior—then bolted out of his home, running all the way across town to tell Brown. "Hallelujah!" shouted the surprised pastor, unable to contain his joy. "Unction can be transmitted!"

The First Radio Church

Later, that broadcast of April 8, 1923, would be seen as the first nondenominational religious service ever carried by radio. But for Brown, it was the unexpected start of an exciting new gospel outreach. Encouraged by response to his initial message, he accepted the offer to become the regular pastor of WOAW. The arrangement was unusual. In all his years, no contract was ever signed, no salary ever paid. Brown kept the work separate from his regular services at the Omaha Gospel Tabernacle. And he insisted his Sunday "radio service" be aired before most church services began, to avoid any conflict.

Not trusting the mechanical equipment to carry his voice across the prairies, he shouted at the microphone. He gestured to his unseen audience, envisioned the holes in the microphone as his listeners. As the work grew and letters arrived by the bag, Brown had a novel notion. He'd heard from families who could not get to church because of rainy season roads, and from congregations without pastors who met around the radio for their Sunday morning sermon.

Listeners looked to him for pastoral teaching and guidance, wrote to him for prayers and counsel over their personal trials, and told him how God had blessed their lives. He began to see his *Radio Chapel Service* audience was really a new form of church. With that idea, he sought ways to meet the spiritual needs of his scattered flock—to be more than just a voice on the radio, but to get involved in their lives and to get them active for the kingdom.

At last Brown worked out a method. Listeners would be invited to join the "World Radio Congregation" and issued official membership cards. United into a cohesive organization, his audience could then be mobilized to raise funds for disaster relief and to pray for others to trust Jesus Christ as their Savior.

The World Radio Congregation took off like a shot! In two years, by 1925, listenership had soared to more than a hundred thousand. Within a decade *Radio Chapel Service* enjoyed a weekly national audience of more than half a million people. Brown himself gained a reputation as the "Billy Sunday of the Air," pastor of America's first radio church. But he never did stop shouting at the microphone.

An Unhappy Beginning

Henry C. Crowell was glad he had stuck it out and gotten his engineering degree from Yale. When the transmitter towers were installed at Moody Bible Institute of Chicago, as the new station manager he was able to personally supervise their construction. When the school asked the federal Department of Commerce for a license to operate its own radio station, he was able to guide the application through the maze of paperwork and technical issues.

Once the license arrived in July 1926, the new WMBI was ready to take the airwaves. It hadn't been easy, though. Moody Bible Institute had been raising the necessary funds for more than a year. Some contributors were still a bit skeptical about radio, but most were cautiously excited. Crowell counted himself among that group. Harnessing this miracle of technology, he believed, was in the best spirit of D. L. Moody's original mandate "to effectually teach and preach the gospel of Christ."

And of course, radio had shown it was here to stay. Crowell had seen the national excitement Paul Rader was creating across town in his broadcasts from the Chicago Gospel Tabernacle. Across the country, at least sixty churches and religious organizations now operated their own radio stations. And since earlier that year, when two Moody music students filled in for a local radio program, response was so great that the school was now broadcasting two hours of music and lectures six evenings a week.

That July, Crowell counted down the days until it was time for the big opening broadcast. The whole school had been buzzing about it for weeks. The inaugural broadcast of WMBI was an important event and all the top leaders of Moody Bible Institute were eagerly awaiting the occasion. He was determined that, from an engineering standpoint at least, he would not disappoint them.

As the first WMBI program signed on the air July 28, 1926, everything seemed to be going great. The program manager, Wendell Loveless, had put together a fine gospel program. An accomplished composer of sacred songs, he had an obvious talent for radio from the start. He worked as announcer, pianist, vocalist, and Bible teacher—wherever he was needed. Loveless poured himself into the radio ministry. As Crowell watched his colleague at work, he knew WMBI would reflect the special talents and creative ability of its program manager for years to come.

For now, though, Crowell had his own concerns. The hookups and amplifiers and transmitters were all working properly. So Crowell relaxed a bit and allowed himself a smile. Those months of sweat and hard work were paying off. As he turned back to his work, however, someone was trying to get his attention. Something was going horribly wrong! People were tuning in their radios, but the signal was having trouble getting through. Crowell frantically checked over his equipment, hoping to find the problem. What was going on?

Chaos and Competition

Though nothing turned up wrong, it didn't take long to discover the real problem. Another radio station had been licensed to the same wavelength and was broadcasting its own inaugural program at the same time as WMBI! Crowell was dismayed. As station manager and engineer, he tried to keep on top of developments in the radio industry. He was well aware that radio had grown so far, so fast, it had outpaced the few government regulations in place to control it. But this was ridiculous!

In just a few short years, Crowell had watched an amateur hobby become a routine part of American life. More than five million homes now owned radios. And not jerry-built crystal sets, but ready-made units that ran on household electrical current rather than leaky batteries, and looked like home furniture rather than laboratory equipment. Yet as sets became more sophisticated, it was harder than ever to pick up an intelligible signal. Stations changed frequency, increased power, and went on and off the air whenever they wished. Bedlam reigned over the airwaves. The new medium of radio was rapidly choking itself to death.

Each year since 1922, the government had called a National Radio Conference to discuss the growing chaos on the airwaves. Crowell followed the meetings closely, including the 1925 conference that asked Secretary of Commerce Herbert Hoover to regulate radio station broadcast times, signal strengths, and frequency assignments. In 1926, President Calvin Coolidge urged Congress to take action, and lawmakers responded with the Radio Act of 1927 that established a new Federal Radio Commission.

The FRC was authorized to issue licenses, allocate frequencies, and limit power. Almost immediately, the new agency took action. It declared the airwaves were public property. Government must ensure they would be used for the public interest, which "is of superior importance to that of the broadcaster." Thus the Commission believed "it is better that there should be a few less broadcasters than that the listening public should suffer from undue interference." The FRC was true to its word. Within months, one out of every five radio stations in America—about 150 of the 732 stations on the air in 1927—relinquished their licenses.

Mr. Crowell Goes to Washington

The long journey by train from Chicago to Washington gave Henry Crowell time to think. He hadn't planned on the trip, but neither had he expected yesterday's surprise telegram from the Federal Radio Commission. "Power increase absolutely out of question and cut in power may be necessary," read the terse Western Union wire, "[so] please consider this situation carefully before making final conclusion." Consider carefully? Final conclusion? Crowell knew only too well what the Commission was driving at. Signal interference was a concern shared by all. But the FRC's solution, as the telegram seemed to insist, was that WMBI cut its broadcast hours and share time with several other Chicago stations.

Of course, Crowell had expected stiff questions in applying for the station's 1927 license renewal. The federal agency had taken several religious stations to task for "not serving the public good," for being "propaganda" outlets that allegedly benefitted only a small segment of the public. The FRC was even threatening all religious stations with exile to the remote end of the AM radio band.

As the train prepared for its final push into Washington's Union Station, Crowell once more went over his case. In their first year on the air, Crowell and program manager Wendell Loveless had guided WMBI as a nondenominational, educational radio station. Strong propaganda and direct financial appeals were avoided. Slanderous statements attacking other religious viewpoints were prohibited. Guest speakers were chosen with care and strictly warned against careless comments. As a result, no formal complaints had ever been lodged against the station. In fact, after receiving a personal letter from the president of Moody Bible Institute, WMBI supporters had sent the FRC more than fifty thousand postcards urging renewal of the station's license.

Those postcards must have impressed the Commission, because when Crowell and his two Moody Bible Institute companions arrived in the nation's capital, they quickly won a private audience at FRC headquarters. In keeping with his engineer's training, Crowell's approach was logical, dispassionate, and well prepared. He laid out the facts and avoided dramatics as he demonstrated a keen knowledge of the radio industry and a sympathy for the agency's concerns. "Would it not be possible," he asked the commissioners, "to allocate a small number of wave channels to be used jointly by educational and religious stations? The channels could be suitably located, not at the remote end of the present band, but where they would be of service to the average listener."

After deliberating, the FRC unanimously agreed WMBI was "operating in the interests of public convenience, interest, and necessity." The agency approved a new wavelength on the growing AM band, then a month later assigned WMBI a frequency of 1140 kilocycles that it had to share with only one other station. (The Moody outlet ultimately was granted an exclusive frequency in 1941.) Crowell was certainly glad to be among the survivors. Over the next three years he made ten trips to Washington. But even as much as his personal visits helped, it was clear Washington had taken a new attitude. Radio was no longer for preachers who swept church floors by day and took a microphone at night. The game was being played by new rules, and religious stations must be run as professional operations to survive.

First-Class Failure

Lois Crawford was not happy. She had gotten all the books about radio that she could find at the library. She had even *bought* a book!

Then after studying for weeks and weeks, she had driven all the way to Chicago for her exam. These days the government required station operators to get a First Class Radio Telephone License. But when the test scores came out, she had flunked. And even worse, she had missed by only a few points.

Of course, a year ago Lois didn't even know such a thing as a First Class Radio Telephone License existed—much less how to get one. It was only toward the latter part of 1926 that the Crary Hardware Store in Boone, Iowa, let it be known they wanted to sell a 10-watt radio station. They were asking $150. That was a lot of money! But they said the station was fully licensed. Nobody in town wanted it. The newspaper turned them down. Might be more competition, the owners said. Then someone had a sharp idea. "There's a man in west Boone who likes to preach. Maybe he'd take it."

That man was her Papa, Charley Crawford, a Congregational preacher from Kansas whom God had called to Boone in 1891. Since then he had established a church, along with the Boone Biblical College, Christian Boarding School, and Boys Home. When he proposed to buy the radio station, Lois disapproved. For one thing, Papa wanted to put the transmitter in the church basement. That was such a dark and gloomy place to be! And he wanted to broadcast from three to four on Sunday afternoons, just when Lois was teaching Sunday school at a mission church across the river. It was springtime and she loved the walk. But Papa insisted. In fact, he couldn't even wait to move the equipment—though you could carry it in a wicker clothes basket. So on January 25, 1927, he turned on the transmitter at Crary's Hardware Store. KFGQ was on the air! Lois was assigned to listen on the radio from the college. "Was that singing," she asked Papa later, "or was it a tin can banging against the wall?"

Soon after buying the station, one of the Crawfords' former students heard about the new venture and sent four thousand dollars in government bonds. That was more money than Lois had ever seen at one time! Now KFGQ could afford to buy some new parts and make some needed repairs. One of Lois's boarding school students was interested in radio engineering and volunteered to help. For advice, he borrowed a bicycle and pedaled fourteen miles over to Ames. There he looked up the engineer at WOI, the radio station at Iowa State University. The man was sympathetic and drew a wiring diagram, then offered some spare parts he didn't need.

The station generator needed a new motor, so the students took one from an old broommaking machine. Then the radio tubes needed a battery to work, so they got one out of an old Dodge. At last they strung the antenna from the church steeple to the top of the Boys Home. But Papa had to hire a student from Iowa State University, one who had a First Class Radio Telephone License, to operate the station. Lois groaned every time a paycheck was made out. It was outrageous to pay him five whole dollars just for one hour of work each Sunday. "If that pink-cheeked boy can get a license," Lois declared, "so can I!"

Lois didn't make it the first time around. But three months later she took the examination in Chicago again. This time she passed with flying colors. Later somebody told her she was the first woman in the United States to earn a First Class Radio Telephone License. That was nice, but Lois was mostly glad that KFGQ could keep on broadcasting the gospel of Christ. Some people told Papa that, with only 10 watts, the station would never be heard outside of town. But that was all right, Papa replied. "There are plenty of sinners in Boone!"

God Shuts a Door

Along with WMBI and KFGQ, other gospel broadcasters worked hard to meet the new technical standards of the Federal Radio Commission. Many important stations were successful in keeping their licenses and later developed large audiences. These included KFUO/St. Louis, begun by the Lutheran Church Missouri Synod in 1925; KPOF/Denver, operated by the Pillar of Fire denomination since 1928; and KFSG/Los Angeles, founded in

1924 by evangelist Aimee Semple McPherson and her Church of the Foursquare Gospel.

Other religious broadcasters were not prepared to keep up with a rapidly changing industry. Most stations operated only on Sundays, airing worship services or other church events. For only a few hours of broadcasting once a week, it was difficult to justify the expense of purchasing the power modulation equipment required by the FRC or of hiring licensed radio operators. Other station owners simply lacked the time or knowledge to keep up.

For its part, the Federal Radio Commission soon made it clear that noncommercial stations would be second-class citizens of the airwaves. The agency allocated only limited hours of operation to noncommercial broadcasters, mostly during the daytime, effectively removing them from competition with commercial stations. Frequency assignments were changed, abruptly and arbitrarily, as the FRC deliberately made room on the dial for new commercial operators.

One agency commissioner put it this way: "Commercialism is the heart of broadcasting in the United States. What has [noncommercial] education contributed to radio? Not one thing. What has commercialism contributed? Everything—the lifeblood of the industry." Year by year, religious radio stations were going off the air. Between 1927 and 1933, the number of stations licensed to religious groups declined from about sixty to less than thirty.

God had seemingly closed a door. While a few evangelical groups would continue to operate their own stations, direct ownership of radio by religious broadcasters would not (for now) become the mass movement that men like Paul Rader had once envisioned. In the new era of commercialism and government regulation, churches and religious groups could not compete. But as God was closing one door, he was opening another—to a way of proclaiming the gospel on a scale never before imagined.

2

THE NETWORKS RISE

1927–1943

When Walter A. Maier called on the Columbia Broadcasting System, he had a vision. Any other man would have had little hope. Yet five years of broadcasting had given him a growing excitement about what he called "the miracle of radio." Now in 1929, Maier was convinced the time was right for a nationwide program "preaching an authentic Christianity." In less than two years, not one but *two* national radio networks had suddenly burst upon the scene. They offered a national outreach his small Missouri station could never match. Brimming with confidence and purpose, he made the rounds of the network offices. And now he was no longer so certain. One network had already turned him down, and the other was asking him to do the impossible.

Maier remembered his reception some weeks ago at the National Broadcasting Company. He had gone there first because NBC was the largest radio network in the nation. Executives were friendly and polite, impressed with his sincerity and integrity and broadcast experience. But, they told him, the network simply did not sell time to religious broadcasters. It's nothing against you, they said, just a matter of policy. Discussions were amiable, but they would not budge.

Instead the network invited Maier to consider a request for sustaining time. NBC was donating airtime to the three major faiths, with Protestant participation arranged by the Greater New York Council of Churches (a task relinquished in 1934 to the Federal Council of Churches). The policy was worked out in 1928 for the NBC series *National Radio Pulpit*, the first religious broadcast to originate from a network studio. And the policy clearly stated that religious groups should receive free time but pay their own production costs, and messages should be nonsectarian, "avoiding matters of doctrine and controversial subjects."

Of course, evangelical denominations such as Maier's Lutheran Church Missouri Synod (LCMS) were not represented in the theologically liberal Council. But the NBC executives suggested a short segment might be made available. They were outwardly positive, but Maier knew the network could pull the plug whenever it wished. Compared to the Council of Churches, the LCMS was only a small religious body with little clout.

Things weren't much better at CBS, the newest of the two national radio networks. Executives were preparing a policy against paid religious programs—a response to the politicized radio preaching of Father Charles Coughlin—and planned to allow only nondenominational broadcasts during sustaining time. Until the guidelines were adopted, however, the network was willing to sell time for one more half-hour program—at a cost of two hundred thousand dollars for one season. Maier was staggered! That was an unimaginable sum of money! How could he possibly raise so much? And yet Maier knew if he failed to act now, CBS would soon shut the door. Only sustaining time programs would be aired and his vision of preaching "authentic Christianity" to a national audience would come to nothing. This might be his only chance. Could he take such an incredible leap of faith? Radio listeners wanted lively programs, news, and entertainment. Most people would say that thirty minutes of unvarnished preaching and church music had no chance to attract an audience. That's what the network executives expected. Was he foolish, or even vain, to think he could succeed? Two hundred thousand dollars was, after all, an enormous commitment.

Forward, Upward, Onward

As he looked over the CBS contract, Maier remembered the first time he faced a radio microphone. It was seven years ago, in 1922, at the annual Walther League convention in Louisville, Kentucky. What a time that was! Maier was twenty-nine years old then, had graduated from seminary and been ordained, earned his master's degree in Old Testament and Semitics from Harvard, and was then elected in 1920 as national leader of the LCMS youth league.

He was slated to bring the keynote address, and when a local radio station offered to broadcast the speech, he gladly agreed. Maier had always been impressed by the potential of mass communication. That was why he agreed to serve as editor for *The Walther League Messenger*, which had since become one of the largest evangelical publications in America. The last seven years had seen many changes in his life and ministry, but editing the newspaper remained close to his heart.

After the 1922 convention, Maier stepped down as executive secretary of the Walther League. He would soon be thirty and it was time to establish his career. When he was offered a professorship at his old alma mater, Concordia Seminary of St. Louis, Maier accepted. But though he had a turn for scholarship, the Lord had also given him a growing burden for proclaiming the gospel through the marvel of mass communication. Not long after his arrival at Concordia, he met a young engineer who was interested in radio. In 1924 the two men approached the seminary president with an idea.

If the administration would agree to having a radio station on campus, Maier would raise the funds. As editor of *The Walther League Messenger* he would appeal to the newspaper's readers for support. The seminary agreed, the funds were raised, and by December 14, 1924, the new station was on the air. The day of the first broadcast was bitterly cold, but Maier's spirits were undaunted. He predicted it was "only the beginning." When the government assigned the call letters KFUO, Maier declared the new radio outreach would "Keep Forward Upward Onward!"

The next four years were busy ones for the Old Testament professor. His Hebrew class was reputed to be the largest in America. As his reputation developed, he became in great demand as a conference speaker. He continued to edit the *Messenger* and at the same time completed the rigorous requirements for a doctoral degree in Semitic Studies from Harvard University. Yet he was always at the microphone for his two weekly radio programs on KFUO. For most men, this would be enough. But Maier was never a man to be satisfied. He saw that America, sickened by the endless killing of the Great War, had drifted away from the old values. The people had plunged into the new "anything goes" society with a vengeance. As respect for law and order had declined, crime and immorality had run rampant. And the growing threat of communism loomed above the horizon. The nation needed a call to revival and Maier was convinced that God, in this moment of history, had provided "the miracle means" of radio.

Who Won the Rose Bowl?

The "miracle means" of national network radio had been emerging since 1922, the same year Maier was heard on the airwaves from the Walther League convention in Louisville. The introduction that year of the superheterodyne receiver was a widely heralded breakthrough. But the true birth of commercial radio was hardly noticed by the public at the time.

Since the federal Department of Commerce had begun issuing licenses in late 1921, most new permits had gone to colleges and universities for educational programs, farm news, and weather reports. Many other stations were run by newspapers—or by makers of radio sets, mostly to sell their wares. As the medium spread, however, new station operators sought a better way to ensure financial stability.

An answer came on August 28, 1922. That summer a New York real estate firm had tried, unsuccessfully, to sell two buildings in the borough of Queens. The company got in touch with WEAF, a new station in the city, and offered to pay for a program if the station made an announcement about the two properties for sale. The advertisement was aired, the buildings were quickly sold—and with that first sponsored program, commercial radio was born.

A month later another New York station, WJZ (later WABC), teamed with WGY in upstate Schenectady for an experimental joint broadcast of the 1922 World Series. Another early network test, linking stations in New York, Washington, and St. Louis, carried a 1923 speech by President Warren Harding to an unprecedented audience of more than one million people.

Harding's death later that year shocked the nation. A network of seven stations was quickly assembled so that America could hear its new president, Calvin Coolidge, address the Congress. Limited "chain" broadcasting, as it was called, aired the Democratic and Republican conventions of 1924. After Coolidge was reelected, two dozen radio stations carried his 1925 inaugural address by transcontinental hookup to more than thirty million listeners.

However, network radio had reached its limit. Though long-distance lines now extended across the country, most stations could not use them. Standing in the way was the giant American Telephone and Telegraph Company, which not only controlled the lines but had a radio station network of its own. All other stations were kept off the lines, unless they agreed to join the AT&T network.

In 1926 the impasse was broken when AT&T left the broadcast business and sold its stations to the Radio Corporation of America. RCA then established the country's first regular radio network under the name of the National Broadcasting Company. Its coast-to-coast debut, aired over nineteen stations, came on New Year's Day 1927 with a play-by-play broadcast of the Rose Bowl game from Pasadena, California. Yet NBC wasn't alone for long. Commercial advertising was turning radio into a big business. NBC had been on the air a few months when a rival network, the Columbia Broadcasting System, was organized with a basic chain of sixteen stations.

A Turn for the Worse

As a broadcaster himself, Maier had closely watched the development of network radio. He had watched with great interest in 1928 as a pastor from Philadelphia, Donald Grey Barnhouse, became the first preacher to buy network time for a religious broadcast. Barnhouse had first been exposed to radio during a wartime tour in Europe with the Army Signal Corps, and when he accepted the call from Tenth Presbyterian Church, he stipulated that broadcast equipment be installed in the pulpit.

Beginning in 1927 with a local program, Barnhouse ended his first year of broadcasting with a net balance of eleven cents. Yet with faith in God and in the new medium of radio, he signed a forty-thousand-dollar contract with the CBS network for a year of weekly broadcasts. Now his program was steadily gaining new listeners for the gospel and within a few years was being heard on more than one hundred stations across America.

Maier knew the potential outreach of network radio was enormous. Yet two hundred thousand dollars was so much money. Of course, Donald Grey Barnhouse had trusted God for what seemed like an impossible sum. But things had changed. The news from Wall Street on October 29, 1929, had hit the nation like a hard right cross to the jaw. A decade of postwar prosperity had suddenly come tumbling down like a house of cards. Already they called it "Black Tuesday," the day of the Great Stock Market Crash. Now the country was in a depression. It would be tough to raise money for any cause, no matter how worthy. Millions of people, Christians included, had seen their life savings swept away in the financial hurricane. Folks just didn't have any money to give. Yet Maier was convinced that God was using the calamity to get people's attention. He believed their hearts were being prepared for a message of spiritual hope, a message they had ignored in better times. God was in control of the economy, and if he had still seen fit to give Maier an open door for radio, then the Lord would also supply the financial need.

An answer came when the Lutheran Laymen's League, the national organization for Missouri Synod laity, agreed to sponsor the broadcast. The group launched a vigorous campaign in churches throughout the denomination. Within months nearly one hundred thousand dollars was raised. It was only half the total needed for the year, but it was enough to get the program started. Maier took it as a sign to proceed, trusting the Lord to build a listening audience that would support the broadcast with its contributions.

That There Is a God

On a chilly Thursday night, October 2, 1930, listeners across the country tuned in *The Lutheran Hour* for the first time on the CBS radio network. Since the KFUO studio at Concordia Seminary was too small, Maier had arranged to broadcast from station WHK in Cleveland. He planned a brief opening announcement, then ten minutes of classical church music by the Cleveland Bach Chorus, concluding with a nineteen-minute sermon from the Word of God.

When the day of the broadcast arrived, the choir members straggled into the studio one by one, lining up around the microphones as the engineers instructed them. Maier checked over his notes, then looked up as the announcer was cued and *The Lutheran Hour* was on the air! As he expected, the musical portion of the program went off without a hitch. Maier smiled to himself. He had chosen well. The music of the Cleveland Bach Chorus was certainly an inspiration.

To Maier, the minutes went by swiftly as the chorus finished its program. When they were done, he was already at the microphone waiting for his cue. The engineer pointed as Maier silently cleared his throat and faced his unseen audience. From the beginning he wanted listeners to know where he stood and boldly proclaimed that his opening message was dedicated "to the fundamental conviction that there is a God."

As the broadcast continued, Maier warmed to his message. He had preached over the radio now for six years and knew how to handle a microphone. And for this broadcast he was even more prepared. He could see the audio engineers wince as his voice ranged from a soft conversational level to thundering decibels. But the country needed conviction, and with God's help, he was determined to give it to them! Finally, as the program drew to a close, Maier addressed himself to a nation that was struggling desperately for answers in the depths of its greatest depression.

"In the crises of life and the pivotal hours of existence," Maier told his audience, "only the Christian—having God and, with him, the assurance that no one can successfully prevail against him—is able to carry the pressing burden of sickness, death, financial reverses, family troubles, misfortunes of innumerable kinds and degrees, and yet to bear all this with the undaunted faith and Christian confidence that alone make life worth living and death worth dying."

When it was over, Maier went over to thank the chorus and engineers. And silently he thanked the Lord for allowing his vision to become a reality. Maier knew the Lord would use the broadcast to make a difference—and he was soon proven right. In just eight weeks *The Lutheran Hour* surpassed all mail sent to programs sponsored by the Federal Council of Churches, including the four-year-old *National Radio Pulpit* that featured such prominent and theologically liberal speakers as Harry Emerson Fosdick, S. Parkes Cadman, and Ralph W. Sockman. The volume of letters even surpassed those of popular entertainment programs such as *Amos 'n' Andy*.

By the end of the season, CBS estimated *The Lutheran Hour* was reaching a national weekly audience of more than five million listeners. That was a stunning outreach for a small denomination whose total membership was less than two million. Contributions from listeners averaged two thousand dollars a week, enough to sustain the broadcast. Skeptics were dumbfounded that a simple program of singing and preaching could achieve such rapid success. But letters from pastors and laity of all denominations praised *The Lutheran Hour* for its clear message and emphasis on traditional Christian beliefs.

Most listeners attended church regularly, but many turned to Maier for biblical teaching they didn't receive from their own pastors. Others wrote to say *The Lutheran Hour* had led them to Christ or had turned them back to God. Church life in the United States had become spiritually dull, but Maier's "vigorous reassertion of classic Christianity" had come upon America like a new breath of life.

A Mighty Voice

Even as *The Lutheran Hour* was preparing to debut, across the country God was raising another champion who was destined to be linked with Maier as the two greatest gospel radio voices of their generation. But in September 1930, Charles E. Fuller was mostly worried about the hot weather in Los Angeles.

He was anxious to get back on the air after being forced to cancel his radio programs for the summer. That February he had arranged with a new educational station in Santa Ana to broadcast Sunday morning services from Calvary Church, where Fuller had been pastor since 1925. In May the church purchased more time for a youth-oriented musical program that allowed listeners to phone in Bible questions for Fuller to answer live on the air. When attendance at Calvary soared to standing room only, however, the sweltering heat forced Fuller to stop the radio programs until the church could improve its facilities for broadcasting.

Stopping the programs was a hard thing for Fuller to do. A year ago, in 1929, he had made God a solemn promise. It was in Indianapolis, after the annual Defenders of Christian Faith Conference, where he had shared the platform with his old mentor Paul Rader. At the last minute, a local religious radio program needed a substitute for its regular speaker, and Fuller agreed to help. His message wasn't much, just a short sermon from Mark 4:35–41 about the stilling of the storm on the Sea of Galilee. He had preached on that passage many times before. A few days later, however, the station called him. They said his message had generated an unprecedented volume of calls and letters from listeners who said the message had impacted their lives. They had never seen any response like it!

On the long train trip back to California, Fuller had time to think. It had been a great conference, full of great preaching and fellowship. But his thoughts kept returning to that radio program. As he thought and prayed, Fuller felt moved by the Holy Spirit to make a promise. God was giving him a burden to use radio as a "mighty voice" for reaching the "vast multitudes who needed to hear the gospel." And in that moment, Fuller promised the Lord he would begin preaching regularly on the radio.

Yet he was also humbled, knowing it was God and not himself who would make this outreach possible. Fuller wryly admitted he was probably the most unlikely preacher in the whole state of California. Yes, he had grown up in a Christian home with parents who took him faithfully to church. After graduating from Pomona College in 1910, he joined them in the family orange-growing business and even became an officer in his parents' church. Business success and public respectability were great—except when he admitted the truth. Something was missing in his life.

That something was Jesus Christ. Fuller had never put his trust in the Lord. The years brought him prosperity and things like a good home and even a car. Yet he felt empty inside. He was nearly thirty and, in 1916, it seemed his life held little meaning. Then he heard Paul Rader was preaching at the Church of the Open Door in Los Angeles, and on a sudden impulse, he decided to go.

Fuller had never heard such preaching before! His need was clear, and so was his answer. When the service was over he went outside into the warm California sun. Unable to contain himself any longer, he knelt down beside his car and prayed to be saved and used of the Lord. The change in his life was instantaneous! The old feelings of emptiness were gone, replaced by an overflowing desire to serve the Lord and share his Word with others.

Within a few weeks of his conversion, Fuller organized an adult Bible class at Placentia (California) Presbyterian Church and himself enrolled at the Bible Institute of Los Angeles (now Biola University). Over the next three years he studied hard, earned his Bible degree, but later resigned from Placentia over church doctrine. Nevertheless he kept on, continuing his Bible classes, starting a program over commercial radio in 1923, and teaching a series of Bible lessons over the Biola station in 1924.

The Most Natural Thing

By 1925 the adult Bible class he had led for so many years had grown into the nucleus of Calvary Church. Fuller was called and ordained to be its first pastor, and in the ensuing years he developed a growing reputation throughout the West Coast as a dynamic revival speaker. Now the Lord had given him a burden for radio—and he had a promise to keep.

When Fuller had the chance to keep that promise in February 1930, God had blessed the radio outreach. The summer cancellation was a reluctant decision but necessary. Now in September the church was ready to broadcast over KGER, a much larger station in Long Beach that expanded the church's weekly audience to fifteen thousand listeners. "It just seems the most natural thing in the world," Fuller believed, "for me to tell the Good News of Christ into a microphone, which would wing my voice to an audience many times the size of what I could ever have visibly present."

Three more years of broadcasting followed, twice each week from Calvary Church. But division was growing. While God had given Fuller a vision for spreading the gospel by radio, church officers believed traditional evangelistic methods and local ministries should be emphasized. They desired "to put the church program on the basis of strict economy," as the board minutes recorded.

Sadly, Fuller submitted his resignation in 1932. He would close out his pastorate the following spring with a grand finale series of revival meetings, then launch an independent broadcast ministry supported by listener contributions. But the transition proved far from easy. All the property he had acquired in business, along with property his wife had inherited, had been lost to the depression. His young son had been ill for three years. Yet through it all, Fuller saw the hand of God at work teaching him to "rely solely on the Lord."

That lesson seemed to be serving Fuller well when he set the date of his first independent broadcast: Sunday, March 26, 1933. Over the years he had developed a good relationship with KGER, so it was easy to put things in place for his new program. He was confident that, once on the air, God would move his listeners to provide the needed financial support. With the election of President Franklin Roosevelt, people hoped for change so the country could get back on its feet. In fact, the inauguration was set for March 20, the Monday before Fuller's first broadcast of *The Pilgrim's Hour*, and he planned to take some time off to listen.

The Shock of His Life

It turned out to be a week he would never forget. On Monday, President Roosevelt used his first day in office to close the nation's banks. Nobody knew how long the "bank holiday" would last, so people would be reluctant to make donations. On Saturday, the day before Fuller was to go on the air, an earthquake tore through Long Beach and left 115 people dead. Then Sunday morning, as he drove downtown for his broadcast, U.S. Marines were guarding the city from looters and stopped him from entering the KGER studios. Only when Fuller explained his purpose, and the soldiers saw the Bible tucked under his arm, did they let him in. During the program, Fuller felt a powerful aftershock rock the floor beneath him. He looked out the studio window to see the radio tower swaying dangerously back and forth. And for weeks afterward, he received letters from worried listeners who heard him cry "Look out!" over the live microphone.

From that low point, Fuller had nowhere to go but up. By May, listener contributions for his two programs were running slightly ahead of costs. Fuller established a nonprofit corporation, the Gospel Broadcasting Association, and added a third program in November. For 1934, a fourth broadcast from KNX/Hollywood was put on the schedule. Since the station could be heard in eleven western states, plus Alaska and western Canada, Fuller decided in 1935 to expand the KNX program to a full hour. When he arrived at the cavernous Hollywood studios for his first sixty-minute broadcast, however, the preacher found only fifty people in the auditorium. For music, he asked for volunteers from the audience, and a twelve-voice choir was quickly rehearsed to open the first *Old-Fashioned Revival Hour*—destined to become the largest network religious program in the nation.

The Golden Age of Radio

Even as *Old-Fashioned Revival Hour* went on the air, vital changes were occurring across the industry that impacted religious and secular broadcasters alike. In 1934 the Mutual Broadcasting System was formed, the first new network to offer real competition since the early days when NBC and CBS were established. Mutual needed revenue wherever it could be found and, unlike its rivals, was glad to sell time for paid religious programs.

But the biggest change of all came from Washington. On June 19 the Congress approved the Communications Act of 1934. As of July 11 the Federal Radio Commission, a temporary agency that had to be reauthorized each year, was replaced by a permanent new Federal Communications Commission. While the FCC quickly took an activist stance on the side of the listening public, the agency brought stability to an industry that had operated by haphazard rules and regulations. Where the old Radio Commission had little staff or funding, the new agency was backed by the full weight of government.

With maturity came a "golden age" in radio. Jack Benny, Rudy Vallee, Burns and Allen, Fibber McGee and Molly, Edgar Bergen and Charlie McCarthy all became household names. Commentators such as Walter Winchell, Lowell Thomas, Red Barber, and Arthur Godfrey gained national followings. Drama came to the airwaves with mysteries such as *The Shadow*, adventures like *The Lone Ranger*, and soap operas from *Young Dr. Malone* to *Mary Noble, Backstage Wife*. Successful formats ranged from children's programs (*Little Orphan Annie* and *Jack Armstrong*) and quiz shows (*Can You Top This?* and *The $64 Question*) to popular music (*Make Believe Ballroom* and *Lucky Strike Hit Parade*).

The great era of radio also meant a growing outlet for the gospel. The roll of evangelical broadcasts that came on the air in those years included: *Radio Bible Class* with M. R. DeHaan; *Back to the Bible* with Theodore Epp; *Haven of Rest* with Paul Myers; *Voice of Prophecy* with H. M. S. Richards, Sr.; *Back to God Hour* with Henry Schultze and Peter Eldersveld; *Heaven and Home Hour* with Clarence Erickson; *Bible Fellowship Hour* with T. Myron Webb; *Radio Revival Hour* with Glenn Tingley; *Radio Bible Hour* with J. Harold Smith; *Church by the Side of the Road* with Edna Jean Horn; *Word of Life Hour* with Jack Wyrtzen; and *Right Start for the Day* with Dale Crowley, Sr.

Walter Maier, after suspending *The Lutheran Hour* for three seasons, returned to the air in 1935 from the studios of KFUO and was soon distributed on Mutual Broadcasting network. The program went on to become the largest radio broadcast venture of its time, aired on more than twelve hundred stations worldwide in thirty-six languages with an estimated audience of nearly seven hundred million—perhaps a third of the world's entire population.

In 1937, a management change at KNX forced Charles Fuller off his home station, so he switched to a thirteen-station hookup on the Mutual network that reached as far east as Gary, Indiana. But a new crisis developed eight months later. A large corporation demanded Fuller's time slot for a nationwide program. "Rudy," he told his radio agent, "you let Mutual know that the *Old-Fashioned Revival Hour* will take that network coast to coast." The astonished agent asked if he could afford it, but the evangelist replied, "No, I cannot, but God can!" The cost of airtime jumped from $1,441 to $4,500 a week, but he had made no mistake in trusting the Lord. "Each Sunday by God's grace," Fuller declared to his first nationwide audience, "we have an hour to broadcast the old songs and the old gospel which is the power of God unto salvation. Our one message is Christ and him crucified, and we endeavor by God's grace to beseech men and women to be reconciled to God in Jesus Christ."

Within six weeks of delivering that ringing declaration, the number of stations had grown from thirty to eighty-eight—and by 1939 the *Old-Fashioned Revival Hour* was heard on all 152 affiliates of the Mutual Broadcasting System, reaching an audience of ten million listeners. And while broadcasting on MBS, Fuller still preached every Sunday morning on his local program, *The Pilgrim's Hour,* where he was joined by a live audience. When the weekly gathering outgrew the KGER studios in 1939, Fuller moved the broadcast to the cavernous Long Beach Municipal Auditorium. Three years later *The Pilgrim's Hour* became a nationwide Mutual broadcast, along with the *Old-Fashioned Revival Hour.*

At the peak of his radio ministry in 1943, Fuller was heard on more than a thousand stations at a cost of about thirty-five thousand dollars per week. That year the Gospel Broadcasting Association was the top broadcaster on the Mutual network, and its $1,556,310 of airtime was fully 50 percent more than the next largest secular customer.

Yet Fuller always insisted, "I'm not interested in figures. I'm interested in souls. Some people say I reach twenty million people. I don't know. All I know is that I preach the greatest message in the world. There may be greater orators, but nobody can preach a greater message because I preach from the world's greatest Book. . . . It is the old gospel, the simple gospel that pulls."

For the Duration

But even as Fuller and Maier and others brought the gospel outreach to new heights, the golden age of radio—when stations and programs proliferated with dazzling speed and diversity—was drawing to a close. The United States was at war again. Within months after Pearl Harbor, radio and all areas of communication were put under the jurisdiction of the newly authorized Defense Communications Board. Soon afterward, the FCC ordered a freeze on broadcast assignments and barred construction of new stations for the duration of the war.

And in a blow to every radio preacher in America, the Mutual Broadcasting System in 1943 announced restrictions on paid religious programs that would make it virtually impossible for radio preachers to survive on the air. Thus the old network outlets were cut off, and new outlets were banned "for the duration." If the war ever ended, maybe things would get better. Maybe a new era of gospel radio would begin. But evangelical broadcasters would have to fight for it!

3

THE BATTLE RAGES

1943–1950

J Elwin Wright was used to traveling. Evangelistic campaigns, Bible conferences, literature crusades, radio broadcasts, musical tours. He didn't mind if the New England Fellowship couldn't always pay its founder and president a full salary. God had given him a bookstore and real estate business to provide his needs. And today the businesses could almost run themselves, so he could devote more time to the ministry. But lately, Wright admitted, he had been on the road even more than usual.

Only a month ago, April 1942, he was in St. Louis. There he played a key organizing role as fellow delegates founded the National Association of Evangelicals for United Action. Now he was speaking for the new group at a highfalutin university confer-ence, trying to convince a room full of professors why evangelical preachers should be allowed on the radio. The networks listened to these academic types, so it was important for broadcasters of the gospel to be represented.

Wright had to admit the tidy lawns and landscaped grounds of Ohio State University were attractive. Columbus was a lovely col-lege town and in the first week of May, spring flowers were appear-ing. In his heart, however, Wright was a simple preacher who longed for the rugged White Mountains of New Hampshire. The cool woods near Rumney, the small village where his Bible con-ference met each summer, was always a welcome haven for getting close to the Lord.

If any of those professors thought he was out of place on a big-time campus, Wright wasn't worried. They were probably right! Yet he knew his role as a spokesman for the evangelical cause was no fluke. The Rumney conferences had been bringing evangeli-cals of all stripes together since 1929. In time the meetings coa-lesced into the New England Fellowship and its summer confer-ences became an informal meeting ground for leaders from across the country. Men such as Walter Maier, Charles Fuller, and Don-ald Barnhouse were often booked for NEF events, and Wright gained both valuable contacts and a growing reputation. The talk in Rumney was often about the need for a united evangelical voice on the national level, and in 1941 the NEF board of directors authorized its president to "take immediate steps . . . [to] bring into existence a central and representative organization." And that's when all the traveling began!

His first stop was Chicago, where Wright met at the Moody Bible Institute with an invited group of selected evangelical leaders, including broadcasters Fuller and William Ward Ayer, for a "round-table discussion," October 27–28. Wright shared his vision for a national cooperative association, and the men decided to call an organizing conference next spring in St. Louis. For his part, Wright was named to head a "temporary committee for united action" and was soon headed off across the country to recruit delegates for the April meeting.

Defeated for Decades

As he toured the country that winter of 1941–42, Wright found evangelicals across America were ready to join hands and fight. For a generation they had been tarred with the brush of the 1925 Scopes Monkey Trial and marked as opponents of "progress." They had watched as modernists who rejected the Word of God gained ascendancy in society. At last through radio, the evangelical movement had found a way to reach the public with the life-giving message of salvation in Christ. And just as the gospel was going out across the land, the modernists were trying to pull the plug—and were close to succeeding! When delegates gathered at St. Louis' Hotel Coronado on Thursday, April 7, 1942, keynote speaker Harold John Ockenga quickly captured the mood of the audience.

"Evangelical Christianity has suffered nothing but a series of defeats for decades," declared the pastor of Boston's Park Street Church. "The programs of few major denominations today are controlled by evangelicals. Evangelical testimony has sometimes been reduced to the witness of individual churches. . . . Evangelicals have been so frozen out . . . [as] one by one, various forces have discredited or attacked them, or even forced them out of positions of leadership, until today many of them are on the defensive or even the decline. The hour calls for a united front for evangelical action."

In the early days of radio, stations eagerly sold time to preachers because they needed money—from any source—to get established in the market. Now that radio was a major industry with national and local advertising, it simply did not *need* preachers anymore. Preachers were risky. They made station owners nervous. Could they be counted on to pay their bills? Who could figure the way they raised funds on "faith"? Was it even ethical to ask for money on the air? And weren't some of them crooked—or worse yet, controversial?

Everyone in the country was talking about a Roman Catholic priest, Father Charles Coughlin, who had amassed a national network audience of forty million listeners. He had turned from religion to politics, from anti–New Deal to pro-Nazi, and railed against United States entry into World War II as a "British-Jewish-Roosevelt conspiracy." Finally in 1942, the Vatican had taken the extraordinary step of forcing him off the air. It was better—and certainly safer—most stations thought, to keep away from preachers and stick with conventional advertising.

Made in Heaven?

Then along came the Federal Council of Churches with an answer that, for the networks, seemed made in heaven. Why not let the Council take all the responsibility? Airtime for religious programs would be donated as a public service. The Council of Churches, as the representative body of American Protestantism, would coordinate distribution of sustaining time to its members. It would ensure that program time was allotted fairly across the denominations, given to "responsible" broadcasters—accountable to the Council—who would address the broad public rather than a narrow sectarian view. Donated time would also help stations meet the public service requirements for their license renewal. And by ending the practice of selling time to religious broadcasters, networks would avoid the troublesome questions surrounding independent radio preachers.

The two largest networks, NBC and CBS, had already adopted this policy. Now the Federal Council of Churches focused its attention on the Mutual network. At first the new MBS stations had needed revenues from radio preachers to gain a foothold in the market. But by 1942 the company was well established and less dependent upon money from the sale of airtime to evangelical broadcasters.

Leading the charge against paid religious programs was the Institute of Education by Radio. In 1941 the academic organization had established a committee to study religious radio. Quickly it became an ally of the Federal Council of Churches, issuing proposed network guidelines that struck directly at gospel programs such as the *Old-Fashioned Revival Hour* and *The Lutheran Hour*.

Evangelicals across the country were deeply worried. If Mutual adopted the IER policies, all three major networks would be virtually closed to gospel preachers. Individual stations might follow suit rather than risk their network affiliation and the advertising and programming support that came with it. Now was the time to take a stand! The Institute would be meeting to review and finalize the guidelines during its annual conference, May 3–6, 1942, at Ohio State University. The National Association of Evangelicals was less than a month old, but Wright was dispatched to be its spokesman.

To Be Taken Seriously?

More than 150 evangelical leaders had turned out in St. Louis the previous month, and the session was everything Wright had hoped for. Delegates voted to form a national organization, and a constitutional convention was called for the following spring in Chicago. In the meantime, the battle over religious radio would not wait. He made his reservations for the IER conference and hoped for the best. Yet until he arrived in Columbus, Wright would have no idea whether the Institute would take him seriously or not.

To his relief, he was invited to address the Institute session on religious programs. Sustaining time would continue no matter what action was taken on paid broadcasts, so Wright spoke to that issue first. He rose to his feet, fixed his gaze on the assembled academics, and explained what had taken place in St. Louis. There was a new kid on the block, he declared, and to achieve "a fair division of time between representatives of the principal faiths

. . . we believe there should be *four* rather than three faiths taken into consideration."

In addition to the Catholic and Jewish faiths, Wright went on, "we have two great divisions of the church, probably of approximately equal numerical strength. The first is represented by the Federal Council of Churches of Christ in America. This includes the so-called liberal or modernist groups. The second is the evangelical or conservative group which, up to the present time, has been without cohesion and consequently without representation. The National Association of Evangelicals for United Action seems likely to become the representative of this group of between fifteen and twenty million church members, including practically all Protestant groups not in the membership of the Federal Council, also a large number of individual churches within denominations which are members of the Federal Council but not sympathetic to its program."

After urging that NAE be a "fourth force" in the allocation of sustaining time, Wright focused his remarks on four Institute proposals that dealt with paid time: (1) that all broadcasts should be addressed to "a cross section of the public . . . [and] not to members of any one faith"; (2) that paid religious programs should be eliminated; (3) that only sustaining time broadcasts should be allowed; and (4) that solicitation of funds on the air should be prohibited.

While Wright could "heartily agree . . . religious programs should not attack the beliefs of members of other faiths," he explained that the first IER recommendation would so dilute religious content that programs would "cease to have the power to bring conviction of spiritual need." NAE would find this unacceptable, he told the audience, for "we believe that this is a matter of eternal life or death, whether men accept Jesus Christ as Deity and the only Savior of mankind. Believing this, we would be lacking in sincerity . . . if we failed to do all in our power to win men to faith by the preaching of his gospel." In fairness, he added that evangelicals would equally defend the rights of Catholics and Jews "to be just as positive in their programs as we wish to be in ours."

Elimination of paid religious programs, Wright went on, had been done at NBC and CBS with the practical effect of "almost entirely exclud[ing] . . . doctrinally conservative groups." Even if NAE were treated as a "fourth force" in distribution of sustaining time, he pointed out, "the broadcasting companies are not likely to be willing to contribute the amount of time which the presentation of religion deserves and requires. We believe that groups financially able to carry a broadcast should be permitted to buy time."

And if a broadcaster is paying for time, Wright urged, "it is only reasonable that opportunity be given to the listeners to share in the expense." Audiences tune in gospel programs—voluntarily—for spiritual benefit and may rightly be asked to share the expense through free-will donations, in the same way churches invite worshipers to contribute.

"There is undoubtedly a good deal of racketeering going on in connection with religious broadcasts," Wright admitted to the IER session, but "that racketeering is almost wholly confined to a certain type of program which is undesirable from every standpoint." Evangelicals are "desirous of giving full cooperation in curbing such programs," he said, perhaps by requiring broadcasters to obtain certification according to standards set by NAE or their respective church councils. But he candidly suggested the proposed solicitation ban was aimed "not only against racketeering broadcasters but [also against] others which provide no reasonable ground for complaint."

In the end, the Institute of Education by Radio rejected Wright's argument and endorsed a ban on solicitations. But he was encouraged by the conference agreeing that NAE should have a fair allotment of sustaining time, that some paid-time slots should be preserved, and that evangelicals had a right to broadcast their convictions "without dilution." Since IER was a private organization, its guidelines were not binding on stations and networks but carried the force of "expert" consensus. In his report to the NAE executive committee, Wright declared that these gains showed "the vast amount of constructive work which may be accomplished" now that evangelicals "are in a position to speak through a central organization."

Different Directions

Elwin Wright had arrived on May 3, 1942, for the opening of the IER conference. One year later, to the very day, he joined more than a thousand Christians in Chicago for the constitutional convention of the National Association of Evangelicals for United Action. What a difference a year made! The organization had come together in a wonderful way, and by the time delegates left Chicago they had approved an ambitious agenda for missions, evangelism, education, military chaplain recruitment, and government relations. Wright himself was commissioned to lead the new staff—and raise the money!

No one appreciated the efforts of Wright more than James DeForest Murch, the young and dynamic speaker on radio's *Christians' Hour*. The NAE Chicago convention was an exhilarating event, and Murch was thrilled to be part of history in the making. But even as he joined delegates in applauding the new group's aggressive agenda, in the back of his mind he had a nagging concern.

There was a great need for united evangelical action in many vital areas, especially now that the war was impacting everything from missionary travel to ministerial draft deferments. Yet the issue that had first galvanized the movement, the threat to gospel broadcasting, had grown more dangerous and complex as the year went by. It was no longer a matter of simply voicing evangelical arguments for academics who had never heard them before. Now it was a matter of exercising real leverage and doing real battle. NAE was being pulled in many different, and important, directions. Could the association muster the concentrated effort needed at this crucial juncture for religious broadcasters?

Murch knew that the Mutual network, focus of the Federal Council of Churches campaign, was wavering. The modernist press was in headlong attack led by its flagship journal, *The Christian Century*, which opened with a salvo against "the network religious program racket, capitalized by independent super-fundamentalist revivalists" who "have long been distasteful to [progressive] church leaders, to much of the listening public, and to network officials." The council then mounted a frontal assault, signing more than fifty radio stations to "ironclad contracts obliging them to use the Federal Council approved programs and no other," and vowing to enroll every radio station in America.

At last in the fall of 1943, the Mutual Broadcasting System gave way before the modernist assault. Like evangelicals across the country, Murch was utterly dismayed. The network announced restrictions on paid religious programs that made it virtually impossible for radio preachers to survive. Broadcasts would be confined to Sunday mornings only and limited to no more than thirty minutes, with no direct solicitations for funds allowed over the air. Charles Fuller, for example, would be forced to trim his two one-hour programs, *Old-Fashioned Revival Hour* and *The Pilgrim's Hour*, and accept only a single half-hour morning broadcast. And Walter Maier, who had moved his program from CBS to Mutual some years ago, would have to reduce *The Lutheran Hour* to thirty minutes. Many other gospel preachers would be forced off the air.

An Effective Pressure Group

Murch was incensed. An accomplished writer, as well as a broadcaster, he rushed into print with articles and editorials condemning the Federal Council of Churches for its policy and the Mutual network for its action. And he was not alone. The MBS announcement sparked a spontaneous nationwide protest from the evangelical community. Reaction was intense and immediate. Some groups held mass meetings and mounted high-powered publicity campaigns to castigate MBS and the Council of Churches. Others urged legal action and unrelenting war.

But as he thought about such tactics, Murch became uneasy. He believed those in positions of authority with the government and radio industry wanted to be fair-minded and public-spirited. From their viewpoint, the ban on paid time was a rational response to a thorny issue. To impugn them in public as "enemies of religion" would only drive them away in alienation. Better to work with the networks in a constructive way, Murch thought, to earn their respect and show how gospel broadcasters could meet their concerns if paid programs were reinstated.

But how? To be credible, the effort would need the support of the National Association of Evangelicals. Through his involvement with the NAE radio committee, Murch knew the association would do whatever it could to help. Yet with NAE occupied by so many other vital concerns, how could a sustained and effective campaign be mounted to lobby the networks and counter the powerful Federal Council of Churches?

Murch was thinking the matter over without much success when the telephone rang. To his surprise, on the other end of the line was Eugene Bertermann, business manager for Walter Maier and *The Lutheran Hour*. He had read Murch's articles and really appreciated them. Would Murch be available to meet with Dr. Maier in Cincinnati later this month? Murch stammered out his agreement and then hung up. He wondered what might come of it, but sensed the hand of God was at work.

On the day of the meeting, the three men met early at Cincinnati's Gibson Hotel. Right away, a great rapport sprang up between them. Maier and Bertermann were visibly impressed with the clarity and conviction of Murch's writings and his grasp of the issues. They needed an ally in the fight to keep *The Lutheran Hour* on the air and believed Murch could be a vigorous proponent for the evangelical cause. Despite Maier's busy schedule, they spent the entire day discussing every phase of the controversy. Bertermann even offered to provide copies of his correspondence with MBS and the

Federal Council so Murch could use them to further publicize the issues.

As the day grew late, the room stuffy, and the hotel chairs uncomfortable, the three men turned to ideas for what to do next. Quickly they came to an agreement. They would approach the National Association of Evangelicals with two requests. First, they would ask the organization to "go to bat" for *The Lutheran Hour*. The effort was ultimately successful, since NAE retained some of the nation's finest communications lawyers to win assurances that Maier could remain on the air. Their second request, however, went beyond *The Lutheran Hour* or any individual radio program. The three men would urge, as Murch said, that NAE sponsor a "move for the organization of all evangelical broadcasters into an effective pressure group which could deal officially with all the broader and deeper problems involved."

Amid Hopeful Signs

Radio was a large and complex industry, now under wartime rules that made things even more complicated. Religious broadcasters could not afford to assign others to fight their battles for them. So Murch was glad when NAE agreed to hold a meeting of gospel broadcasters in conjunction with its second annual convention slated for April 1944 in Columbus—the same city where Elwin Wright had won their first victory at the Institute for Education by Radio. Now two years later, Murch felt that broadcasters were meeting amid some other hopeful signs.

Of course, keeping *The Lutheran Hour* on the Mutual network was a big boost to everyone's spirits. It showed what could happen once industry and government leaders were calmly acquainted with the facts. Charles Fuller had also been given a year's grace by MBS, until the start of the 1944 season in September. He was using the time to line up a national network of independent stations to carry the popular *Old-Fashioned Revival Hour*—setting a pattern many radio preachers would follow in the years to come—while keeping the new thirty-minute *The Pilgrim's Hour* on the Mutual system. By announcing the new lineup months in advance, Fuller hoped, and ultimately proved, that listener response could remain near its 1943 peak.

The simple fact that religious broadcasters were now gathering to form a united front, Murch thought, was the most hopeful sign of all. Some 150 broadcasters turned out on April 7, 1944, for the two-day radio session of the NAE convention. Yet despite the optimism, there was no hiding the grim reality. Hundreds of stations had turned away from paid religious programs, and dozens of preachers had been shut off the airwaves. Once the meeting was gaveled to order, therefore, the broadcasters quickly got down to business.

The Birth of NRB

The first order of business was selecting a temporary president. Pastor William Ward Ayer, who broadcast from New York's Calvary Baptist Church, was chosen to lead the meeting. Then Dale Crowley, Sr., of Washington, D.C., speaker for *The Right Start for the Day*, was named secretary to record the session. Discussion went back and forth, but soon the consensus was clear. When Pastor Vincent Brushwyler of Muscatine, Iowa, stepped forward and moved that "we form a national association of gospel broadcasters, to be affiliated with the National Association of Evangelicals," the response was a ringing "Aye!"

Murch realized, however, that this was the easy part. Now the delegates must decide their strategy, how they would mold an unorganized group of independent preachers into a cohesive and effective lobby. To his relief, the conference put aside unessential differences and adopted a statement of faith that emphasized fundamental doctrines and proclaimed the Bible as the inspired Word of God. Then Murch joined in as delegates approved a new name, National Religious Broadcasters, suggested by secretary Dale Crowley.

The new association would need a constitution and bylaws, and Murch agreed to chair a drafting committee. The panel would submit its draft at a constitutional convention to be held at Chicago in September. The task of developing a code of ethics, one that would promote high standards and reassure the industry and public that evangelical broadcasters could use the airwaves responsibly, was assigned to a committee headed by William Ayer.

The historic session then adjourned and, in the weeks that followed, the committees moved quickly to their tasks. News releases were sent to all stations, networks, industry groups, and government agencies announcing the formation of National Religious Broadcasters and explaining the place of evangelicals in the Protestant church. The most capable communications attorney in the nation, Louis G. Caldwell of Washington, was engaged to counsel Murch's committee in drafting the new constitution and bylaws. And Rosel Hyde, chief counsel and later chairman of the Federal Communications Commission, was recruited to assist in developing the NRB code of ethics.

At last everything was ready and a constitutional convention was called for September 21, 1944, at Chicago's Moody Memorial Church. As delegates assembled in the cavernous auditorium of the historic church, President Wil Houghton of Moody Bible Institute, the unofficial host of the meeting, suggested all discussion be put aside for the moment. "Let us give ourselves," he said, "to prayer." On that day, National Religious Broadcasters was literally born in prayer as delegates each brought the new organization before the Lord according to their own manner of praying. "The very presence of God," said one awestruck broadcaster, Glenn Tingley of the *Radio Revival Hour* program, "seemed to come down upon us."

Down to Business

When the business of the convention was opened, the constitution was presented for adoption. The preamble of the document forthrightly declared that National Religious Broadcasters would be "a corporation of doctrinally evangelical individuals concerned for the spread of the gospel of our Lord and Savior Jesus Christ . . . banded together for the sake of the strength which comes from numbers united in a common cause. Thus united, the religious broadcasters feel they can contribute to the improvement of religious broadcasts, better serve the interest of Christian people, and more effectively minister to the spiritual welfare of the nation."

The code of ethics developed by Ayer's committee was incorporated into the constitution and written in two parts: a section for producers of radio programs and another for station owners and operators. The code covered issues of sponsorship, character, production, cooperation, advertising, financial accountability, regulatory compliance, and responsibility to uphold the gospel, the family, and the nation. The association would endeavor, under its new code of ethics, to "establish and maintain high standards with respect to the end that such programs may be constantly developed and improved, and that their public interest and usefulness may be enhanced."

By acclamation, the new constitution was approved. In accordance with its provisions, Ayer and Crowley were confirmed by election in their offices of president and secretary, while the posts of vice president and treasurer went to Clinton H. Churchill of station WKBW/Buffalo and broadcaster David J. Fant of New York. A board of directors was created with rotating three-year terms, and among the familiar names appointed to serve were Walter Maier, Theodore Epp of *Back to the Bible*, and M. R. DeHaan of *Radio Bible Class*.

To provide responsive leadership, a select group of board members were appointed to an executive committee to serve along with the national officers. Here the new association sought to establish a tradition of enlisting the most distinguished names in religious broadcasting. Murch and Tingley were named, along with Myron F. Boyd of *Light and Life Hour*; Paul Myers of *Haven of Rest*; Charles Leaming of *Faith Gospel Broadcast*; John Zoller of *Christ for Everyone*; Bob Jones, Sr., founder of Bob Jones University; Thomas F.

Zimmerman, later the general superintendent of the Assemblies of God denomination; and Torrey Johnson, later the founder of Youth for Christ.

The exact relationship with the National Association of Evangelicals was left open, as Murch explained to others, to be "worked out in later conventions." On December 18, 1944, National Religious Broadcasters was awarded its charter of incorporation by the state of Delaware. In time the new group emerged as a separate corporate identity. Religious broadcasting, which had once been a primary concern of NAE, now shifted to broadcasters themselves. The one-time parent organization would remain a supportive observer, but for better or worse NRB was on its own.

Postwar Radio Boom

With the end of the Second World War in 1945, radio communications were returned to civilian control. The Federal Communications Commission, which three years earlier had placed a freeze on licenses, now opened the floodgates of radio to a nation that was eager for entertainment. By the end of 1945 more than a thousand stations were licensed, and an estimated 93 percent of American households owned a radio—up 20 percent from before the war. And a new national network, the American Broadcasting Company, came on the scene in 1945 when the federal government forced NBC to divest one of two networks it owned.

FM operations, which had been authorized in January 1941 but frozen a year later, were now given a more desirable part of the radio band under an FCC plan to eventually accommodate fifteen hundred new commercial FM stations. Space on the dial was also reserved for noncommercial stations, which had been virtually regulated out of business during the late 1920s by the old Federal Radio Commission. Now such stations, including those owned by churches and religious groups, could make a comeback.

The stakes for evangelical broadcasters in this new postwar market were enormous. The potential for proclaiming the gospel was expanding geometrically. To be shut out by the networks and the National (formerly Federal) Council of Churches and their policies against paid religious programs would be unforgivable! So the leadership of National Religious Broadcasters moved decisively on two key fronts.

Its first campaign was to ensure that gospel preachers obtained a fair share of sustaining time from the networks. "After many months of correspondence and conference," recorded Murch, "understandings were reached which fully protected the rights of all accredited (by NRB) religious broadcasters at national and local levels. The distinctly evangelical testimony was assured a voice on the air. The National Association of Evangelicals was given its proportionate share of sustaining time on all the national networks, and evangelicals were recognized as having a valid claim to consideration at the local level."

However, when it came to the second front of securing the right to purchase airtime, the NRB strategy required much thought. Some wanted to emphasize the issue of First Amendment rights and pursue appropriate legislation in Congress. Yet that promised an uphill battle against powerful industry lobbies, and if NRB were defeated, the issue would remain dead for many years to come. Others asked if a compromise allowing some paid programs could be worked out with the National Council of Churches. The networks would surely listen if both groups approached them with a united proposal. But in the end, NRB decided the slow but steady work of making its case to the industry, of educating executives and station owners about the issues, and winning their respect was the best strategy of all.

Steady Wins the Race

At last, in 1949, the strategy started to pay off. The newest radio network, ABC, became the first to reverse its policy and accept paid religious broadcasts. That year ABC signed up Charles Fuller's *Old-Fashioned Revival Hour*, which drew a weekly audience of twenty million listeners well into the next decade. By outpacing all other religious broadcasts and even the majority of secular daytime programs, *Old-Fashioned Revival Hour* provided a powerful argument against those who claimed only sustaining time broadcasts would be broadly accepted by the public.

Over the coming years, other networks followed. Time on local stations became increasingly available. Radio was proliferating at a rate not seen since the "golden age" a generation ago, and the gospel was going out as never before. For NRB, gains and losses lay ahead as networks often took one step back for every two steps forward. But by uniting their voice, gospel broadcasters had secured their position. No longer would anyone suggest that questions about religious radio could be decided without the evangelical viewpoint. The battle seemed to be won—when suddenly and without warning, the voice of gospel radio suffered a tragic and irrevocable blow.

4

THE PICTURE CHANGES

1950–1957

W hen the news went out on January 11, 1950, millions of radio listeners were shocked. Each week they had looked to Walter Maier and *The Lutheran Hour* for inspiration from the Word of God. Now, suddenly, at the age of only fifty-six, he was gone. And nowhere was his untimely and unexpected loss felt more keenly than among broadcasters. For a generation they had looked to Maier as their champion. At the time of his death, he had preached to more people than any man in history. His support was the linchpin that gave National Religious Broadcasters its start. But just as NRB was winning the battle to keep the airwaves open to the gospel, the evangelical voice had lost its greatest messenger.

Theodore Elsner knew what was at stake. To much of the listening public, Walter Maier *was* evangelical radio. He was a national figure, respected and admired, and his stature had given radio preaching a good name. What use was access to the airwaves, Elsner thought, without the effective testimony of men like Maier? Elsner himself had been broadcasting nearly as long as Maier, since 1931, when he launched the first daily Bible broadcast in the Philadelphia area from his pulpit at Gospel Tabernacle. But he readily admitted that, in the public mind, it was the reputation of Walter Maier that helped set the tone for every other broadcaster.

That year, when Elsner became the third NRB president after Clinton Churchill, he believed one of the vital issues facing broadcasters was the vacuum left by the loss of Maier. The thought was on his mind that summer of 1950, when Elsner decided it was time for a vacation. He knew a small cottage that was available for rent in Ocean City, New Jersey. The beach would be just the break he needed from the city. So he drove in early one morning to spend some time alone with the Lord before the family arrived. And as he prayed, pouring out his concern for replacing the leadership of Walter Maier, he felt a clear conviction that God was impressing a name upon his heart

This Must Be God's Doing!

Ocean City was indeed a delightful resort, and the Methodist camp meeting center there was a peaceful and quiet retreat. William Frank "Billy" Graham was glad to be there. And these days he had more speaking invitations than he could possibly handle! Ever since last year, when the 1949 Billy Graham Los Angeles Crusade had drawn over three hundred thousand people, he had, to his great surprise, become a national celebrity. Later he found out that publishing mogul William Randolph Hearst had ordered his newspaper empire to "Puff Graham." Almost overnight he was hounded by enthusiastic reporters and photographers. His picture appeared on the covers of *Time*, *Newsweek*, and *Life* magazines. And as the publicity helped generate a growing national excitement, the crusade was extended from a three-week event to an eight-week triumph.

Now Graham was big news and grateful for the chance to spend a quiet week in Ocean City. He even had the chance to slip away one morning to play a few holes of golf with his associate, Cliff Barrows, and another friend from the conference. It was great to get outdoors, to enjoy the sea air and summer sun! And to top off a great morning, the three men drove down for lunch to a little diner on the edge of town for some good food and quiet fellowship.

Graham and his two companions were happily shooting the breeze over in a corner of the diner. The rest of the world, including reporters and admirers, seemed far away as they talked about golf and family and old times. Then out of the corner of his eye, Graham spotted a man coming toward them. Tears filled the man's eyes and he was obviously in the grip of some great emotion. He walked straight to their table and, as Graham wondered what the man could want, he blurted in a loud voice, "This can only be God's doing!" There was confusion for a moment; then the man introduced himself. His name was Theodore Elsner.

The Turning Point

When Elsner had finished praying that morning in his rented cottage, he had gotten in his car and driven down to the diner for lunch. Even behind the wheel, he was still in an attitude of prayer, asking the Lord who could fill the shoes of Walter Maier as a national voice for the gospel. Then as he walked into the diner, Elsner couldn't believe his eyes! It was Billy Graham, the very name God had placed upon his heart! Of all the places in the world, at that day and hour, Graham was in Ocean City in the little diner on the edge of town.

Elsner explained that he was president of National Religious Broadcasters and a radio preacher for nearly twenty years from Philadelphia. Then he shared his burden and his definite conviction that this meeting was ordained of the Lord. Now it was Graham's turn to get excited. Soon he was pacing up and down the diner, peppering Elsner with questions about how to get started in network radio.

Graham was not, however, a newcomer to the airwaves. In 1943 the Wheaton College graduate was called to a small church in Western Springs, Illinois. But Graham was well known in evangelical circles, in part because his father-in-law, L. Nelson Bell, was a prominent former missionary to China and now an influential religious publisher. After a year in the pulpit, Graham was tapped by Chicago broadcaster Torrey Johnson to take over his local *Songs in the Night* program as Johnson devoted his time to organizing the Youth for Christ movement.

Later Johnson asked Graham to serve as a YFC staff evangelist, marking the start of his career as a crusade speaker. His rise continued in 1947, when he was named president of Northwestern Schools (later College) of Minneapolis. That year the school was licensed to operate a radio station and, after KTIS went on the air in 1949, Graham was a frequent speaker. He even conducted what was later believed to be the first radio "share-a-thon."

But radio on a national scale was something new to him. Graham had seen, through the Hearst newspaper articles and national magazine coverage, how the mass media could energize the outreach of the gospel. And Graham himself was more eager to preach than ever, for the Los Angeles crusade had shown him people "were desperately hungry to hear what God had to say through his Holy Word." He was captivated by the idea of extending that message through network radio. He asked how it could be done, and Elsner gave him two suggestions.

Persistence Pays

The first suggestion was to meet Walter Bennett, a powerhouse in secular radio who had also promoted *The Lutheran Hour* and other evangelical programs. The second was to meet Fred Dienert,

Elsner's son-in-law and partner in the Walter F. Bennett Advertising Agency. Graham thanked him for the reference and, after lunch was over, left the diner with a promise to look into the idea.

Two weeks later Bennett and Dienert introduced themselves to Graham at a Bible conference in northern Michigan and offered to help him start a radio ministry. But in the days since Ocean City, his duties as a college president and conference evangelist had been as pressing as ever. He had quite enough to do and informed the two advertising agents he lacked the time for a regular radio program.

Yet Bennett and Dienert persisted, showing up a week later at Graham's home in Montreat, North Carolina, with some great news. A desirable time slot on Sunday afternoons was available on the ABC network. They could have coast-to-coast coverage for thirteen weekly broadcasts at a cost of only $92,000. Bennett and Dienert were hoping for an enthusiastic response, but they were soon disappointed. "That kind of money I know nothing about," declared Graham, who then abruptly ended the meeting.

Soon Graham was off to a crusade in Portland, Oregon. He was surprised, and somewhat annoyed, when the two ad men kept pursuing him by long-distance telegram and telephone. Bennett and Dienert explained the weekly program cost was only $7,000, that $25,000 was enough to get it on the air, and listeners would pay for the broadcast thereafter. Graham was irked by their talk and said the money was "$25,000 I don't have!" When Bennett and Dienert arrived in Portland, he refused to see them. When they would wait for him in the hotel lobby, Graham used the rear elevator or fire escape to avoid them. When a staff member gave them an appointment, Graham escaped to a nearby resort for a day off. But then the Lord intervened.

Graham received a telephone call that day at the resort. A wealthy friend had heard he might be interested in radio and offered $2,000 to set up a fund. That got Graham to thinking. Was God at work here? He returned to Portland that evening and called Bennett and Dienert over to his hotel room. Was the network's Sunday slot still available? Could wealthy donors be contacted in time to book the broadcast? The two advertising executives told Graham it was risky to depend on "a lot of big people" and instead suggested he take an offering at the crusade that night. At Graham's request the three men knelt in prayer. The evangelist pledged all he owned if God called him to a radio ministry. "But I want you to give me a sign," he prayed, "and I'm going to put out the fleece. The fleece is for $25,000 by midnight."

I'll Grant It's a Miracle

They were pleased when the attendance that night was estimated at more than twenty thousand people. But when the offering was taken, Bennett and Dienert were surprised when Graham made no mention of radio. Only after the offering did the evangelist describe the opportunity in radio. Anyone who would like to take part could see him at the close of the service. When the sum of $25,000 was mentioned, a few ripples of laughter floated out from the crowd. Then Graham finished his sermon and brought the meeting to a close. Bennett and Dienert were glad to see the hundreds of people who streamed down the aisles to receive Jesus Christ as their Savior. But they couldn't help feeling a bit discouraged. Graham would be counseling and praying with the new converts for a long time yet. Few people, they thought, would wait around to see him about a radio program.

Much to their surprise, and to Graham's also, a crush of people were waiting outside the arena office door. When the evangelist arrived, a staff member was holding a shoebox holding cash, checks, and pledges scribbled on crusade programs and songsheets. One businessman said he hoped Graham would pick up the torch left by Walter Maier and pledged $1,000. Altogether the contents of the shoebox, together with the original telephone pledge, came to $23,500.

Bennett and Dienert hailed it as a miracle. But Graham disagreed. "No, it's not a miracle. The devil could send $23,500. It's all or nothing!" The two partners offered to guarantee the last

$1,500 themselves, but the evangelist firmly declined. Downcast, the group returned to the hotel. It was a few minutes before midnight when a staff member brought up three envelopes that had been left at the front desk. Graham opened the first one. It was from a person in another city who felt burdened to start a radio fund so Graham's sermons could be heard regularly over the air. Inside was a check for $1,000.

With a trembling hand, the evangelist opened the next two envelopes. Both were written on hotel stationery, and both contained $250. Now the total of cash and pledges came to exactly $25,000! Graham looked up at the clock, just a minute or two shy of midnight, and exclaimed, "Now I'll grant it's a miracle!" That night there was a prayer meeting, and a few days later the Billy Graham Evangelistic Association was officially incorporated. At the suggestion of Graham's wife, Ruth, the new program was named *Hour of Decision*.

The first broadcast on Sunday, November 5, 1950, originated from the Billy Graham Atlanta Crusade, carried by the ABC network to 150 stations. In a matter of weeks, *Hour of Decision* surpassed the previous all-time high for a religious program, amassing an audience of more than twenty million listeners. That first year more than two hundred thousand letters were received at "Billy Graham, Minneapolis, Minnesota," and by the second year *Hour of Decision* drew larger audiences than the Sunday newscasts. Within five years the broadcast was heard on more than a thousand stations with an estimated audience of fifteen million. No one could take the place of Walter Maier. But God had raised up another to bear the torch, to carry on as a national voice for the gospel.

That same year, 1950, Graham began to explore other ways to use the miracle of media in proclaiming the Good News of Jesus Christ. Even as *Hour of Decision* went on the air, others were going behind the camera to film his crusades and make them into motion pictures and a series of *Hour of Decision* telecasts aired between 1950 and 1954. This was a radically new technique. But as Graham—and a few others—were now discovering, the visual media could be a powerful tool to capture and transmit the preaching of the gospel. The picture of evangelism was changing.

The First Gospel Telecasts

You had to get their attention! If Percy Crawford had learned anything after twenty years of ministry, that was a lesson he would never forget. It was true for adults, and it was true for young people most of all. God had given him a special burden for young people. They kept you on your toes. If your message got stodgy and complacent, they let you know it—with their feet. Crawford had a passionate desire to reach young people with the gospel and would try anything new and exciting that might get their attention. For example, there were the Saturday night youth rallies. That's how, in 1930, his days in the ministry got started. Back then Crawford was a youngster himself, twenty-eight years old, the ink barely dry on his Wheaton College diploma. So he did what came naturally, drawing young people to Jesus Christ through exciting gospel "pep" rallies with lots of hand-clapping, upbeat music, and dynamic, youth-oriented preaching. A year later the rallies grew into the *Young People's Church of the Air,* one of the early gospel programs on national network radio and a success right from the start, expanding to a network of six hundred stations.

As the years went by, Crawford watched as this "Youth for Christ" movement snowballed beyond belief. In 1944 he had preached to seventy thousand young people at Chicago's Soldier Field, the largest gospel youth rally in history. Now the movement was going around the world under the leadership of Torrey Johnson and his staff evangelist, Billy Graham. His own youth ministry encompassed not only youth rallies and radio, but also a camp meeting center in Pennsylvania and The King's College in Briarcliff Manor, New York. Yet in youth work, Crawford knew, standing still was the same as going backward. What was new and exciting? What would get young people's attention?

These days everybody was talking about television. Experts had been predicting a new era for years, but now it looked like the technology would finally come home to the average American. An NBC station, W2XBS in New York, was the first to sign on the air in 1930. But it was President Franklin Roosevelt's televised opening of the 1939 New York World's Fair that really generated excitement—and license applications.

The economic basis of the new medium was assured in 1941 when the Federal Communications Commission gave approval for television broadcasters to accept commercial advertising. The war put television on hold as the FCC froze licenses, banned new stations, and stopped all production of television sets. Once restrictions were lifted in 1945, and the agency adopted standard specifications for television receivers in 1947, the race was on. That year only fifty thousand sets were in use across America; by 1948 another fifty thousand sets were being added each *month*.

W2XBS/New York had presented the nation's first religious telecast on Easter Sunday, 1940. But it was Walter Maier, the greatest voice of gospel radio, who preached the first nondenominational worship service ever seen on television. That year, 1948, the first weekly program of *The Lutheran Hour* fell on New Year's Day, and business manager Eugene Bertermann arranged to have it televised locally over KSD-TV/St. Louis. By the fall of 1949, the development of coaxial cables made network television practical. Crawford was convinced the visual medium was an unparalleled new way to get the attention of young people—and networks offered a way to carry the message.

A Door No Man Can Shut

Prodded by the persistent work of National Religious Broadcasters, ABC had recently become the first network to reverse its policy and accept paid religious programs. With that, Crawford believed the Lord had set before him an open door that no man could shut! He approached the network, persuaded that God had ordained television as a new miracle means for evangelizing the world. Variety shows were a television hit and ABC officials, who needed money and programming, were willing to give Crawford's music-oriented *Youth on the March* a try.

When it went on the air in 1949, *Youth on the March* became the first religious broadcast to appear on network television. The program, originating live from New York each Sunday night, brought top-notch young musicians and speakers to the screen. The young people worked both in front of and behind the camera, and each week their testimonies of the Christian life were all the more compelling because of the visual dimension of television. Viewers had never seen anything like it. The old religion wasn't just for old people! Seeing them live on television, you couldn't deny that here were young people with a faith that made a difference! Within months, *Youth on the March* gained a loyal audience that soon grew into the millions. Percy Crawford had gotten their attention.

Making the Switch

It was television's potential for drama that got the attention of Herman Gockel, editor of the Lutheran Church Missouri Synod magazine who also headed the denomination's 1952 debut of *This Is the Life*. Not one synod official even owned a television set when the board of directors allotted $750,000 for the initial series of twenty-six weekly episodes. The idea of a dramatic program, depicting true stories of men and women saved by Christ, was a radical departure from the aural medium of radio. But Gockel believed television was more truly the daughter of cinema, so that the story itself should carry the audience along. *This Is the Life* premiered September 7, 1952, and ultimately grew from the original four stations to become the most widely telecast religious program of its day, eventually reaching a network of nearly five hundred stations across five continents.

With public acceptance of religious programs such as *Youth on the March* and *This Is the Life,* as well as the weekly *Catholic Hour Broadcasts* that debuted on the CBS network with Bishop Fulton J. Sheen in 1951, evangelicals could recognize the great potential for gospel television. Yet few radio preachers were ready to give the new medium a try. Some wanted to "wait and see" if television would take hold. Others already had large radio ministries and could not afford time for new ventures.

The switch from radio to television wasn't easy. Television production was enormously expensive compared to radio. Video equipment was new and costly. Audiences wanted both sound *and* sight, so professional technicians were needed to ensure a quality broadcast. And the idea of soliciting funds on television seemed somehow inappropriate in a way that did not apply to the strictly aural medium of radio. Then, too, the success of *Youth on the March*— which continued on ABC through 1951—and *This Is the Life* suggested viewers wanted programs with action and movement. Even Bishop Sheen, whose broadcasts were mostly speaking, won audiences by his dynamic on-camera personality. Preachers could not simply transfer their radio formats to the new visual medium— even as many celebrated radio actors and comedians could not transfer their talents to the television screen.

For all these reasons, evangelists making the switch would have to treat television as a completely new and separate ministry from their radio outreach. Some were not equipped organizationally or financially to handle a new venture. Others were not equipped to adapt their style of preaching and presentation. Thus it was a new generation of young preachers to lead the way into gospel television.

In 1952, Rex Humbard believed God was directing him to leave life on the road and establish a nondenominational church in Akron, Ohio. A few years earlier his family, a traveling gospel singing team from Arkansas led by his father, had been the first musical performers ever to appear on the new CBS station in Indianapolis. Now the young pastor's vision for Akron included a television outreach. Funded by his new congregation as a ministry to the elderly and sick who could not attend church, he signed on the airwaves in 1953 over the local Akron station, WAKR-TV.

A year later a friend of his, a young tent evangelist from Tulsa, Oklahoma, named Oral Roberts, was asking Humbard for advice. In 1947 Roberts had narrowly missed an assassin's bullet and media publicity had catapulted his "faith healing" crusades to national prominence. Since January 1954 he had been preaching on sixteen stations but felt the studio broadcasts inhibited his style. The networks refused to produce a live program from his gospel tent, saying it could not be done. But with Humbard's encouragement, he hired a film company for $42,000 and trusted God to give him 420 people who would donate $100 each. Within weeks the funds were raised and, in February 1955, Roberts broadcast the first live tent service ever seen on television.

Back East, another young broadcast pioneer first signed on the air in 1956. Four years earlier, Jerry Falwell would have never been caught in a church. But when his mother left their Lynchburg, Virginia, home each Sunday morning, she turned on the radio really loud. She knew Jerry and his alcoholic father would not get out of bed to turn it off. So she set the dial to Charles Fuller and the *Old-Fashioned Revival Hour*. As the words sank in, Falwell sensed a spiritual hunger. One Sunday night in January 1952, at a new Baptist church in town that was supposed to have a lot of pretty girls, he recognized the gospel message Fuller had always preached and gave his life to Jesus.

Within days of his conversion, Falwell left Virginia Polytechnic Institute, gave up his plans to become a mechanical engineer, and enrolled in Baptist Bible College of Springfield, Missouri. When he graduated in 1956, again it was only days until he was back in Lynchburg, knocking on doors and starting a church in a defunct Donald Duck Bottling Company plant. A week after preaching his first sermon to thirty-five people, Falwell purchased time for a weekly radio program. A few months later he was also broadcasting live every Sunday afternoon from the studios of

WLVA/Lynchburg. As he drove to the station each week along the scenic vistas of the Blue Ridge Mountains, the sky seemed to have no limit. But for the new medium of gospel television, there was a storm brewing on the horizon.

Conviction before Unity

"Why can't you Protestants settle your disagreements amicably with some sort of compromise on broadcasting policies?" Sol Taishoff leaned back in his chair. He was editor of *Broadcasting* magazine, published from Washington as the bible of the industry. All that year of 1956 he had watched these religious types fight each other. National Religious Broadcasters? National Council of Churches? What was the difference? They should just make their peace and be done!

Taishoff looked squarely at the preacher seated in the chair opposite his desk. The man said his name was James DeForest Murch and that he had been elected president that year of National Religious Broadcasters. He had asked for an appointment, and now he was asking for a good word in the magazine! Maybe the issue was worth a few inches. But broadcasting was a big industry. Who wanted to hear some nitpicking little squabbles about religion, about preachers and ministers arguing among themselves?

Yet the man was not put off. "There are several kinds of Protestants," he began to explain, "and we are unwilling to give up our differing convictions for the sake of unity." Well, Murch seemed to have his answers ready. For a preacher he was a cool customer. Taishoff had to give him that much. "May I illustrate?" he continued, and Taishoff waved him on.

"There are several kinds of Jews—Orthodox, Reformed, and Conservative. . . ." But with that, Taishoff had heard enough! Now the debate was hitting home. With a hearty laugh he threw up his hands and told Murch, "You don't need to argue your case any further. I know what you're talking about. You certainly have equal rights before the law, and the sale of time is the easiest way to guarantee those rights." They chatted a few minutes more; then Taishoff called in two of his best reporters. "Hear this man's case," he curtly instructed them, "and pepper him with questions. Then I want you to report the NRB convention for our next issue."

The National Council—Again

Murch was looking forward to the 1956 convention with great anticipation. After a decade of steady progress on the issue of paid religious programs, news had come that the Council of Churches in several states was making a new bid to control Protestant broadcast rights. The furor was sure to guarantee a big turnout for the convention. And Murch scheduled the event in Washington, where NRB's presence could make the most impact.

From his seat on the NRB executive committee, where Murch had served now for a dozen years, he had seen the controversy coming. Murch knew exactly why the National Council of Churches was making its move. For one thing, the rapid emergence of television had breathed new urgency into the debate over religious broadcasting. Two years ago, in 1954, television revenues had finally surpassed radio. (It would take radio another ten years to regain its 1954 level.) And then, as some large NRB members balked at joining the National Association of Evangelicals for fear of losing acceptance in wider Protestant circles, the NCC was ready to exploit the perceived split.

The arguments were the same as 1944, yet this time with a new twist: Religious television programs should only be broadcast on sustaining time, the Council argued, with no fund-raising allowed on the air. Moreover, allotments should be coordinated by the Council to ensure broadcasters are "responsible" and accountable. Yet the group also pointed out that most religious telecasts were of inferior technical quality, a troubling issue in the visual medium of television. So it was further proposed that all Protestant programs be produced under authority of the NCC Broadcasting and Film Commission. It seemed a reasonable plan that would improve technical standards and save money by channeling production costs through a central agency.

Conventional Wisdom

The challenge was immediate, and once elected as NRB president, Murch moved fast. First he contacted broadcasters who had not been active in the association, then reached out to other independent or denominational groups that had hesitated to join before. He launched a monthly newsletter to keep the ranks informed and enthused. The annual convention was moved to a prestigious Washington hotel, where the NAE public relations office could assist in gaining news coverage.

The chairman of the Federal Communications Commission was invited to speak at the convention, along with the president of the National Association of Broadcasters and important network executives. Senators and representatives were invited to a "Congressional Breakfast" that featured a big-name panel discussion on the issues. Exhibits were also permitted for the first time at an NRB convention. And a full slate of technical workshops was scheduled to address the real concern of improving the production quality of gospel television.

When it was all over, Murch was relieved. The NRB Washington convention went over big! He was thrilled to see the great press coverage and gathering momentum NRB would need to win the fight. Then about a week after Murch returned home to Cincinnati came the biggest break of all. He picked up the latest issue of *Broadcasting* and there, inside the spread about the NRB convention, was a boxed editorial by Sol Taishoff. Murch glanced at the page nervously at first. The magazine had such a high standing that its views were the last word in defining the mainstream of industry opinion. As he read on, however, his lips slowly smoothed out into a wide grin. *Broadcasting* had endorsed the NRB cause and was championing the right of religious broadcasters to purchase radio and television airtime! Murch smiled and said to himself, "We've got it made."

Later that year, NBC reversed its ban on selling airtime for religious programs and CBS followed suit a year after. Then, on a miraculous Saturday night, June 1, 1957, all America was transformed into a great gospel tabernacle as Billy Graham preached the first nationally televised crusade ever seen in the United States. Recorded live from Madison Square Garden at the 1957 New York Graham Crusade, the historic series of seventeen weekly ABC broadcasts were a revelation to the entire country. Most viewers had never seen a gospel crusade. To watch normal, average Americans responding to an invitation to be "born again" was a complete discovery. More than 1.5 million letters were sent in. Some 330,000 wrote voluntarily to say they had accepted Christ as Savior. The picture of American evangelism would never be the same.

5

THE MEDIUM MATURES

1957–1978

David Hofer loved to sing. The night was wearing on, but the quartet was going strong. And when they hit a chord just right—well, there was nothing like the feeling of four-part gospel harmony. The only thing that gave him a greater thrill was seeing people come down the aisle once the music and preaching were over. Yet tonight was different. Tonight the invitation was aimed at *him*.

Every gospel rally was special, of course. But Hofer and the quartet had been to revival meetings before. Why had God chosen this night, this place, to move upon his heart? Sure, the Youth for Christ evangelist, Paul Pietsch, was preaching with real power and conviction. That was part of it, he knew, but not all. As Hofer stood on the platform, he felt a growing assurance that the Lord had brought him here, to this town, for an appointment. Dinuba was just a tiny dot on the California map, about thirty miles east of Fresno. It was like many small towns scattered across the vastness of the valley where the quartet had sung before. But as the warm night air of the San Joaquin Valley hung over the hall, mixed with the faint piney scent of the Sierra Mountains beyond, Hofer became certain that here was the place God had called him.

First Commercial Religious Radio

Dinuba didn't look like anyplace special when Hofer had driven up from Los Angeles that day. Like himself, the guys in the quartet were all students at the Bible Institute of Los Angeles. Their thoughts were about getting to the rally, staying on pitch, and returning home to their studies. It was 1945, the war in Europe and Asia was just about over, and young men were looking ahead now to getting an education and exploring the new world that lay beyond. The Youth for Christ rally promised to be exciting, but Dinuba just happened to be a place to have a meeting.

Yet as Paul Pietsch wrapped up his message and issued a challenge, he told a story that got Hofer's attention. In that valley was a group of business leaders who were praying for a revival. They had called prayer meetings across the San Joaquin Valley and had petitioned the Lord for a Christian radio voice that could be heard throughout the region. Was anyone in the audience willing, Pietsch asked, to be that voice? Would anyone take the challenge to begin a radio station in the San Joaquin Valley, perhaps right here in Dinuba? With the war nearly over, the government freeze on new radio stations was being lifted and the number of new licenses was going to boom. Why couldn't any of those new stations be owned by Christians for the purpose of providing airtime for gospel broadcasters?

In a moment, Hofer knew that invitation was aimed at him, that God was prompting him to be that voice in the valley. He looked at the friends standing with him on the platform, but especially at his brother Egon who sang beside him in the quartet. When his brother caught the glance he nodded. Together they slipped quietly to the front, to pray together and commit themselves to the task.

Less than a year later Hofer was praying again. This time he was thanking the Lord. His FCC license had finally arrived and a new Christian radio station, KRDU, would soon be on the air from Dinuba. Not since the early days of radio, before government regulations had driven up the cost and complexity of operation, had Christians owned the means of broadcasting in any significant numbers. Yet the idea of operating KRDU as a *commercial* radio station was something new. Would it work?

The weeks counted down quickly, almost too quickly, as the KRDU launch date approached. To generate income, Hofer sought out producers of "time-tested gospel programs" and found they were very receptive to purchasing time on a station owned and operated by Christians. They had been buying slots on independent secular stations for years, but had no control over the programming that came before and after their broadcasts. A gospel program might be preceded by a soap opera and followed by a variety show! And stations across the country were changing their formats with dizzying speed, often without warning.

With the controversy over paid versus sustaining time, evangelicals often had to plead for crumbs or wrangle with abrupt changes in station policies. The idea of a "Christian" radio station that sold time exclusively to religious broadcasters was intriguing. Radio preachers liked the idea, Hofer found, that they could reach two audiences. Now they could attract not only listeners who tuned in for their specific *program*, but also those drawn by the *station* and its sacred atmosphere.

The First Christian Networks

From the very first, God prospered the ministry of KRDU as the station combined service to listeners and broadcasters while providing a fair return on investment to Hofer and his brother. By 1950 more than ten commercially licensed religious radio stations were on the air and their numbers grew steadily each year throughout the decade. Despite the emergence of television, radio in the United States nearly doubled between 1950 and 1960, from about 2,700 stations to nearly 5,000 stations.

With so many licenses up for the asking, many gospel broadcasters wanted a piece of the action. They already owned one station; why not use that station as a flagship and supplier of programs, then apply for additional stations to create a Christian radio network? In 1954 and 1961, the Pillar of Fire denomination added two stations to what was already the nation's oldest religious network, begun in 1928 with KPOF/Denver. Between 1958 and 1960, Moody Bible Institute acquired three new stations after broadcasting alone over WMBI/Chicago for more than thirty years. And in 1959, Northwestern College of Minnesota and its ten-year-old campus station, KTIS, launched a Christian radio network with the purchase of stations in Iowa and North Dakota. Another pioneer in radio group ownership, John Brown University of Siloam Springs, Arkansas, operated four stations—including, in 1948, the first narrowcast campus radio station in America.

Across the radio dial, the amount of gospel programming increased as each year between 1950 and 1960 approximately ten new stations began airing at least two hours a day of religious broadcasts. And thanks to a 1960 FCC ruling, even more time for the gospel was likely. The Commission ruled that radio and television stations could count paid religious programs toward their requirement to broadcast programs in the public interest. Because station owners were glad to sell slots they had once given away as sustaining time, access to the airwaves was greater than ever.

Supported by Listeners

Harold Camping was a volunteer. He might be president, general manager, and chairman of the board. And outside the San

Francisco studios of KEAR, he might be president of Camping Construction Company. But whatever his other titles might be, he was first and foremost a volunteer. No salary. No benefits. No expense account.

When the Board decided "Family Radio" would be a non-commercial, nonprofit operation, that meant God would have to supply every single minute of broadcast time through the support of listeners. Except that in 1958, Family Radio had no listeners. It had a vision, shared by Camping and his friend, Richard Palmquist. Both men had a burning desire to reach the Bay Area with the gospel of Christ and to energize and equip the local Christian community. For years, they reasoned, radio *programs* had been supported by listeners. Why not a radio *station*? The principle was the same. Listeners could rely on Family Radio for the daily encouragement of Scripture readings, sacred music, prayer, Bible teaching, and counsel. Then in turn, Family Radio would rely on the contributions of local Christians who benefited from this outreach. Consistent programming focused on the sovereignty of God was the key that Camping believed would build a supportive audience.

The concept seemed logical, yet many friends urged caution. Others suggested he forget the whole thing. He was a contractor, a guy who swung a hammer. What did he know about radio? And his partner, Dick Palmquist, he might have a smattering of radio training, but the Alaskan bush was no place like San Francisco!

Of course, listeners had supported radio stations before. Perhaps the first was KFSG/Los Angeles, founded by evangelist Aimee Semple McPherson in 1924. But she had the backing of a worldwide ministry, the International Church of the Foursquare Gospel, to draw upon for listeners and support. Successful nonprofit stations always had supportive organizations already in place. There was WMBI/Chicago, formed under the auspices of Moody Bible Institute. And KPOF/Denver was backed by the Pillar of Fire denomination. Others were supported by churches or Bible colleges. What did Camping have? A construction company? Without the link of

95

a unifying outside organization, Family Radio would be staking its life on an unpredictable "mixed bag" of faceless listeners.

So on February 4, 1959, at precisely twelve noon, people didn't know what to expect when KEAR first went on the air with "The Sound of the New Life." But Camping knew what to expect. He was a volunteer. God had called for a gospel voice in the Bay Area, and he had volunteered to serve. The terms of his enlistment were specific. He would trust, God would supply. And God did. So much did listener contributions surpass expectations that within two years Family Radio could purchase two more stations, KEBR/Sacramento and KECR/El Cajon. Through the next decade Family Radio spread nationwide, averaging one new station every thirty months, a rate of growth unprecedented in Christian network radio.

Alone But Not Lonely

As he picked up the pay phone in the lobby, Marion G. "Pat" Robertson suddenly became much more interested in another conversation—one that was happening just a few feet away.

Only minutes ago, on that morning in 1959, he had addressed the assembled pastors and preachers of the Portsmouth Ministerial Association. At twenty-nine, he was probably the youngest man in the room. But he had an exciting new vision to reach the city for Christ, a calling from God that had led him out from a pastorate in New York to a new mission in the Hampton Roads of Virginia. There was an old UHF television station for sale—cheap—and God had placed in his heart a desire to claim it for him.

The ministers nodded, asked a few questions, then adjourned for coffee. With that, Robertson went out to make a phone call. Yet as he fumbled for the coin in his pocket, he heard another conversation that made him stop. Two of the ministers were speaking together. From their easy tone of voice, they must have come to stretch their legs a minute, get some air. They wanted to relax and talk, discuss what they had heard, and had paid no attention to anyone by the telephone. "Well," said one pastor to the other's hearty agreement, "if we can't stop it, at least we can disassociate ourselves from it."

Robertson put down the receiver in his hand. He was stunned. He had expected the pastors would at least encourage any effort to get out the gospel. And the active help of local churches could be a big boost. Yet he admitted his proposal had problems. The idea of a "Christian" television station was unheard of, and skeptics wondered if he could even get a license. The studio Robertson wanted to buy was a dilapidated and vandalized ruin. Lenses had been ripped off cameras and beer cans were scattered across the floor.

At the time, Robertson himself didn't even own a television. And even if he had, it wouldn't be able to receive the Portsmouth station. UHF channels had only gotten FCC approval in 1952, and thus most television sets were equipped for VHF reception only (an issue not solved until 1964 when Congress mandated that all new sets receive both bands).

Now he faced another decision. Robertson had counted on support from local pastors and churches. Could he go it alone? Yet if God had directed him into television, he was not really alone. Besides, maybe it was better this way. The business and technical requirements of running an independent television station could not easily be squeezed into the local denominational church structure of a single small city. If the Lord had brought him this far, had put on his heart a burden for reaching the lost through television, then "faithful is He that calleth you, who also will do it" (1 Thess. 5:24).

Only What God Told Him

Yet even if he was the son of a prominent Virginia political family and a 1955 Yale University Law School graduate, Robertson confessed the only thing he knew about running a television station was that God had told him to do it. But wasn't that enough? Three years ago, in 1956, he had seen in his own life how God possessed the power to turn anything around. Salvation was the greatest of all blessings, and it had come on the heels of his greatest trial. Robertson had worked hard to graduate from Yale and, when he did not pass the New York bar examination, his dreams for a law career seemed suddenly shattered.

Being the son of a powerful U.S. senator, A. Willis Robertson, only added to the pressure. Success had always come so easily, and now this! Later he became a partner in a New York electronic components firm. But still he struggled with an empty feeling in his life. People always said he had everything going for him. But he didn't look at it that way. For two years, he saw his life in a crisis.

Then one evening Robertson happened to be eating dinner with a missionary from Holland. The young New York electronics executive poured out his heart to this man of God. And when he finished, the missionary replied quietly, "Isn't there something more?" Robertson could think of nothing else to say, though he knew there should be more. Then in a flash of understanding he blurted out, "Yes, I believe Jesus died for the sins of the world—and for my sins too!"

In that instant, Robertson knew he had been converted. Now he belonged to Jesus. Even a famous name and a blue-chip pedigree could never provide the joy and fulfillment that Jesus offered. From then on his course was set. Robertson quit his business, enrolled in the Biblical Seminary of New York (now New York Theological Seminary), and gave himself to serve the Lord. Over the next three years he began to read and pray to draw closer to God, to eliminate things in his life that hindered the spiritual liberty he desired.

Then in August 1959, after his seminary graduation, he was confronted with the matter of his vocation all over again. When his wife and children went to Ohio for a summer visit with the family, Robertson retreated to his New York apartment for a month of concerted prayer. And at the end of that month, he believed God had laid a verse of Scripture on his heart. It was Luke 12:33, which began "Sell [all] that ye have . . ."

What should he do? Then as he pondered, another verse spoke to his heart: "Go home to thy friends, and tell them how great things the Lord hath done for thee, and hath had compassion on thee" (Mark 5:19). With that, Robertson sold his furniture, picked up his family, and went home to Lexington, Virginia. When he arrived, a letter was waiting for him at his mother's house. From out of the blue, a friend from Norfolk whom he had not seen in more than ten years, but who had heard of Robertson's prior business interests in electronics, had written about an abandoned television station in Portsmouth. The idea seemed absurd, Robertson thought. Nevertheless, the friend drove the 230 miles from Norfolk to Lexington to present his proposal.

That night Robertson went out under the stars of the Shenandoah Valley. "Lord," he whispered, "if you want me to buy the station, tell me how much it will cost." After kneeling in prayer, he felt led to offer $37,000. With that assurance, Robertson packed all he owned into a U-Haul trailer and headed down to Portsmouth with his family to possess the station. He had seventy dollars in his pocket.

The Call Letters of God

On January 11, 1960, Robertson filed a charter with the state of Virginia to establish the "Christian Broadcasting Network." His first act as president was to open a bank account with three dollars. His second act was to overdraw that account by ordering a six-dollar checkbook! And the name of the new nonprofit corporation was more a hope for the future than a statement of the present. Robertson did not even have a working station, much less a network! Yet the deal for the station was completed with the help of a major donor who pledged $31,000 toward the purchase price. For now any salary was out of the question, yet the Lord provided an assistant pastorate at a local church to make ends meet.

Receiving an FCC license, however, was no sure thing. Robertson had asked permission to use 50 percent or more of his broadcast time to air religious programs. Never before had the agency considered such a request. If it ever went on the air, the dilapidated old studio in Portsmouth would be the first in America to give a majority of its schedule to religious broadcasts. (The first *exclusively* religious station, KHOF-TV was licensed in 1968 to the Faith Broadcasting Network, formed by Faith Center Church of Glendale, California.)

Robertson knew he was not the first gospel broadcaster to own a television station, because he had been present that day in Philadelphia on July 17, 1960, when WPCA Channel 17 went on the air under the ownership of Percy Crawford. But the station that the evangelist had purchased was a local network affiliate. Tragically, the station failed when Crawford died shortly after its debut. But until then, WPCA was operated as a network outlet, though gospel programs were frequently aired.

Instead, Robertson wanted a license to operate an expressly religious station. Would his application meet FCC standards for serving the broad public interest? He waited and waited, but still no answer came. Months went by. Slowly his request wended its way through the agency bureaucracy in Washington. Then on November 2, 1960, the letter at last arrived. He opened the envelope, nervously at first, then let out a hearty, "Hallelujah!" It was now official! The Christian Broadcasting Network (CBN) had been granted a license!

Dreams of being on the air by Christmas, however, were not to come true. Contributions had fallen behind. The major donor who had promised $31,000 withdrew his pledge. And the FCC said the call letters Robertson requested, WTFC or "Television for Christ," were not available. Discouraged, he considered selling the station to the local school board, a move that would clear all debts and leave a tidy $30,000 profit. Yet even as he went to the FCC in Washington to propose a sale, a letter was forwarded to him from a man who signed himself "A Repentant Procrastinator." "I am a Christian who has been negligent in my responsibility to your effort for Christ," the man wrote, and pledged five hundred dollars.

With those funds, Robertson went back to Virginia and printed thirty thousand newspapers to tell the story of his project. Donations came in. A radio station leased his television tower at a rental that would pay back his entire purchase price in eight years. A pastor appeared at his door who had driven all the way from New York to present him with a check for eight thousand dollars. And two days before the announced air date, a telephone call from Baltimore led to securing five thousand dollars worth of used equipment. In his joy and gratitude to the Lord, Robertson promptly dedicated the call letters the FCC had assigned—WYAH—to the honor of the Hebrew name *Yahweh* for God.

When the day of the first telecast arrived, October 1, 1961, the final equipment payment of five thousand dollars was pledged by a supporter just fifteen minutes before airtime. Broadcasting just six hours a day, the early WYAH operation looked like it had been put together with coat hangers. The signal barely reached around the block—when it worked. Antennas bent with the elements, and it seemed Robertson was always bargaining with bill collectors. But to anyone who asked, he said, "This is what the Lord has provided. It's all his. And if we're faithful with a little bit, his Word says he will trust us with more." CBN was struggling against tremendous odds, he acknowledged, "but I'm trusting in him."

The Most Exciting Event on TV

By 1963, the monthly cost of running the station had hit seven thousand dollars. And CBN had also taken over an old country-and-western radio station, WXRI/Chesapeake, housed across town in an abandoned garage with a seventy-foot antenna atop a creosote pole. Faced with debts that were mounting by the day, Robertson went on the air. He asked for seven hundred people to stand with him, a "700 Club," whose members would pledge ten dollars a month and thereby supply the seven thousand dollars needed.

Response to that first telethon was modest, but God provided enough to keep the station going. Gradually the support of viewers increased. When the 1965 telethon was broadcast, hundreds of callers jammed the studio lines with pledges of support and requests for prayer. The Spirit of God was so evident that others told how they watched at home with tears streaming down their faces. It was the most exciting event they had ever seen on television! A reporter even called the station and asked if it was the second coming of Christ. Robertson told the reporter no, it was just a revival, but he himself knew God had abundantly given the people a spirit of giving.

The next year, *The 700 Club* grew into a daily program—the first Christian talk show ever attempted—with teams of studio volunteers who prayed and counseled with people who called in. The broadcast aired each night at 10:15, often running until two or three in the morning, and hundreds of viewers were led to faith in Christ.

With the 1968 purchase of a second UHF station in Atlanta, Robertson at last put the "network" in Christian Broadcasting Network. That year CBN also broke ground in Portsmouth for the largest television studios in the Tidewater, Virginia, region, with a 10,000-watt transmitter, a $400,000 control room, and a color television production and videotape center to film programs for national syndication. Things were starting to look up for the station that started on a three-dollar checking account!

Technology Claimed for Christ

Innovations in gospel broadcasting were coming so quickly that preachers needed a Bible in one hand and a technical manual in the other. In 1968, evangelist Lester Sumrall and his LeSea Broadcasting Corporation bought a bankrupt Indianapolis station and introduced the idea of "alternative" television, airing family-oriented shows as well as teaching programs. The invention of videotape vastly enlarged outlets for gospel programs;

broadcasters no longer shipped a single film master from station to station but could easily duplicate programs and send tapes to each one.

Cable television, a technology in early use since 1949, was claimed for Christ in 1971 by Redwood Chapel Community Church of Castro Valley, California, operators of the first religious CATV channel in America. That same year, the first religious program ever carried by satellite was beamed via Intelsat IV from the NRB convention in Washington to the Trans World Radio station in Bonaire, for retransmission by shortwave to South America and Europe. But while these vital advances boded a bright future, the public eye was riveted on three pioneer preachers who brought "televangelism" into national prime time.

Three Pioneers Pioneer Again

The television rally had gone smoothly. After fifteen years on the air, Rex Humbard had no greater thrill than to see people come down the aisles to Christ. And that's why he wore a big smile when a businessman he knew came over to shake his hand. The two men talked excitedly together. That year, 1968, a few Midwest stations had picked up his Akron program, *Rex Humbard World Outreach Ministry*, and already response was encouraging. Once the broadcast was aired in all fifty states, a project the businessman had agreed to underwrite, the Lord would do great things. But about that project. Did Humbard have a minute now to talk about it? Just a few details?

Of course, the man was glad to help. No question about that. But he was a businessman. He was "investing" a lot of money and wanted to help make sure the program would be a success. For example, maybe Humbard should make some changes in his program. Just a few things. Not very much. And his nondenominational approach—perhaps the evangelist should take a more specific denominational line. You know, so people can tell where you stand. That wouldn't be a problem, would it?

As Humbard listened, the smile faded from his face. Inside, the evangelist felt a growing sense of dismay. He had already booked time on thirty-three new stations, based on the businessman's promise to cover the deficits until viewer donations at each station could meet expenses. And with those deficits covered, he had made commitments to about sixty stations more. Altogether he had signed up a network of 101 stations! Humbard brought his attention back to the conversation and gently told the man he could not change his message. He hoped the man would understand. In reply the wealthy benefactor quietly mumbled out some regrets and left the rally. Humbard never saw him again.

That set the evangelist to thinking. Everything was in place for a national television outreach. The stations were lined up, the contracts signed, the production arrangements on track. All he needed was the money, and God had been providing that on faith since Humbard—and for that matter, his father before him—had been in the ministry. So he got busy. Within months his Cathedral of Tomorrow church set up a stewardship department staffed with professionals who went out across the country offering various plans for investing in the broadcast. By the end of 1971, *Rex Humbard World Outreach Ministry* was seen not just on 101 stations, but on more than 350 outlets across North America.

In time the Akron evangelist assembled the largest independent network of stations in the world, broadcasting sixty minutes each week in five languages on six continents. His "down home" preaching style and family-oriented musical segments were a hit with viewers the world over. In so doing he brought to the screen a concept, later dubbed the "electric church," pioneered fifty years before by R. R. Brown and the World Radio congregation. The living room sofa could be a pew.

Through television, preachers could build relationships with viewers, get involved in their lives, enlist their support for missionary enterprises. Audiences tuned in the *Rex Humbard World Outreach Ministry* because it seemed like family. Each week they saw the evangelist, along with his wife and children and grandchildren, all reading the Bible together, singing together, listening to stories together. The Humbards made viewers feel right at home—and served them through prayer lines, periodicals, and devotional guides. In turn the television congregation supported an international outreach of gospel tours and missionaries in nearly twenty countries.

Rise Up and Build

And Humbard discovered another fact. In a way radio could not match, gospel television could energize and mobilize its audiences to "rise up and build" (Neh. 2:18). Here was something new. In the early days of mass media, national organizations built national broadcasts. With television, broadcasts could build and strengthen and reinforce a ministry. The visual medium let viewers "get the picture" of a broadcaster's overall organization so that audiences could share in specific ministry projects, as well as pay bills for airtime.

Though Humbard's own plans to fund a new television center and Bible college were thwarted by the government, other religious broadcasters took the cue. In 1969, Humbard's old friend Oral Roberts returned to television after a four-year hiatus with the program *Oral Roberts and You*, enlisting viewers to support the ongoing expansion of his new Oral Roberts University in Tulsa. And across the country Jerry Falwell, after founding Liberty Baptist College (later Liberty University) in 1971, took his *Old Time Gospel Hour* onto national television the following year and rapidly built a dynamic ministry organization.

By the middle of the decade, these three men were national media figures, leaders in religious television. And in the pattern set thirty years before by radio's Charles Fuller, they built national audiences by purchasing time directly from local stations, rather than booking through networks that remained leery of gospel preachers. Buying slots from individual stations gave broadcasters flexibility to select their geographic coverage, to add or subtract stations as finances and priorities dictated.

When America's bicentennial year arrived, Jerry Falwell was appearing on more stations than any other single telecast in America, religious or secular. The Virginia preacher took the name of his program from Fuller's *Old-Fashioned Revival Hour,* and like his old radio mentor he was the top broadcaster of the day. The 251 stations that carried *Old Time Gospel Hour* in 1976 easily outpaced *The Lawrence Welk Show,* the next largest syndicated program with 191 stations. Two years later Falwell was carried by 327 stations across North America, 102 more stations than the entire CBS network. For his part, Rex Humbard amassed the largest independent television network in the world. In 1979, *Rex Humbard World Outreach Ministry* was seen on 237 stations in the United States, 228 in Canada, and 113 more in a dozen different countries. And though Oral Roberts appeared on fewer stations than Falwell or Humbard, his *Oral Roberts and You* featured top musical and celebrity guests that made it the highest rated religious program of the 1970s.

Live via Satellite

Paul Crouch had set the alarm for 4 A.M. With a yawn and a stretch, he rose from the bed in his Jerusalem hotel room. Then he looked out the window. The sky was clear as the eastern horizon brightened with a golden dawn. Good! As founder and president of Trinity Broadcasting Network, he had been planning for this day, May 1, 1977, for months. The first Christian telecast ever transmitted live via satellite! And it would take place from the Mount of Olives, the very place where Jesus one day would return to establish his earthly kingdom. As he dressed, Crouch recited the verse again to himself, "And his feet shall stand in that day upon the Mount of Olives" (Zech. 14:4). The site offered a breathtaking panoramic view overlooking the Old City of Jerusalem. A clear sky would mean great color pictures on KTBN Channel 40 for viewers back home in Southern California.

But at five o'clock it happened. A massive fog bank rolled in, blanketing the city of Jerusalem. Crouch's heart sank as he left the hotel at five-thirty and drove to the broadcast site on the Mount of Olives. There he checked all the final details—sets, camera positions, lighting, microphones. Two Jewish engineers were adjusting connections with the gigantic earth satellite station in the Valley of Elah—the valley where David slew Goliath. And the mayor of Jerusalem, Teddy Kolleck, was on hand to appear as a guest on this historic program. The 6 A.M. broadcast would be seen at 9 P.M. California time. Yet unless God intervened, viewers would see nothing but a thick bank of fog. Crouch looked up at the swirling sky and asked the Lord for a miracle. It wouldn't be the first time! In 1973 he had a secure job in broadcasting. But he sensed God leading him to a new work. Three months later, despite starting with virtually no resources and only a single borrowed camera, TBN was on the air. A defunct UHF channel agreed to sell Crouch airtime until he could buy the station, yet the deal fell through after the transmitter suffered a serious fire. In that bleak moment, however, God provided for the purchase of another station with four times the power and twice the potential audience. A year later the debts were cleared. From then on the station prospered, and at midnight May 15, 1977, KTBN Channel 40 would go on to become the first twenty-four-hour exclusively Christian television station in the world.

The Clouds Rolled Away

It was only ten minutes now until the *Satellite Praise the Lord Television Program* was due to begin. Would God draw forth his hand and roll the fog away? Crouch knew everything was ready; every human preparation had been completed. And the Lord had already done so much to bring them here! For four months he had driven past the big pile of crates in the KTBN parking lot, equipment that could become a satellite dish if only the FCC would grant the permit. At last Crouch decided it was time to get on his knees. That night the regular evening program, *Let's Just Praise the Lord,* was turned into a live three-hour prayer meeting. At midnight Crouch felt his burden lifted, that God had heard his cry. But even he was amazed the next morning when a call came through from Washington. It was his attorney. The excitement in his voice was clear. "Paul, I can't believe this, but we have the construction permit this morning from the FCC for your satellite station! I've never seen anything like it in all my career! This has to be God's miracle!"

Atop the Mount of Olives, Crouch thought about the irony of his predicament. The TBN satellite station had been transmitting now for a month, a gleaming white dish that beamed pictures to a tiny seventeen-foot-long target floating twenty-two thousand miles above the earth. Man could work seemingly great miracles of technology—but only God could roll the fog away! It was now almost six. The countdown had started; tape recorders in Israel and California began to roll. Crouch and his wife Jan, along with the program cast, began to sing the opening theme song, "Let's Just Praise the Lord." The familiar strains echoed across the Kidron Valley, down through the Garden of Gethsemane and past the Eastern Gate. Then it happened! Across the dim outline of the Holy City, the cloud was rolled away.

Success and Survival

By the end of the decade, Jerry Falwell and Rex Humbard were being aired over the largest independent television networks in the nation and the world. The number of television stations with a religious format was growing by one per month, while new Christian radio stations were going on the air at the astonishing rate of one per *week*. Along with TBN, Pat Robertson's Christian Broadcasting Network was also a leader in satellite technology, becoming in April 1977 the first U.S. religious organization to own and operate a satellite earth station. In 1978 two more Christian networks joined the satellite space race, PTL Television of Charlotte, North Carolina, and LeSea Broadcasting of South Bend, Indiana.

Satellites were making it possible for gospel programs to be distributed to far more stations, at less cost, than even by videotape duplication. Within five years TBN was available on six thousand cable channels across America. Viewers could tune in CBN programs via cable television in more than four thousand communities, and PTL broadcasts were offered on three thousand systems nationwide. And a 1978 FCC ruling promised an even greater outreach as the agency authorized the use of small groundbased "translators," fed by satellite, to repeat broadcasts for local television or radio reception. Using a simple $40,000 translator, it was now possible for small towns and rural areas to enjoy their own Christian stations without the million-dollar expense of building a full broadcast facility.

That same year, 1978, the National Council of Churches bowed to reality and endorsed a new policy, that religious groups should have the option to purchase time on radio and television. In the generation between 1959 and 1979, sustaining time had declined from 47 percent of all religious broadcasts to only 8 percent. In 1978 alone, two of the most venerable sustaining programs on television, *Lamp Unto My Feet* and *Look Up and Live*, were canceled by the CBS network after twenty-five years on the air. With old controversies behind and the bright promise of new technology ahead, it seemed nothing now could stop the electric church. However, one more obstacle yet remained. Could religious broadcasting survive its own success?

6

THE WORLD LISTENS

1931–1994

I t was always the same, every morning: Repent your sins, trust in
Christ. Seemed like Paul Rader hardly said anything else. The
preacher called his radio show *The Breakfast Brigade*. No wonder!
He sure gave folks a steady diet of hellfire and brimstone. But Eric
Williams wasn't there to listen. He was there at the Chicago Gospel
Tabernacle each morning to do a job. CBS was paying him to check
the wires, cue the mike, adjust the levels, and engineer the
broadcast. Not to listen. He had enough to do without listening.
Besides, it was always the same. Why, he could just about recite it
himself by now.

Still, Paul Rader seemed like an okay guy. And interesting too.
Used to be a boxer, broncobuster, football player. And you could

tell the preacher really believed what he said. Must be the reason he kept saying it over and over. Yeah, Rader was sincere, all right. Not a phony.

Williams respected that. A lot of those hellfire types on the radio were just in it for the money. And the people around him, they were a friendly sort too. That assistant of his, Clarence Jones, now he was always coming over, talking about radio. Nice guy. Made the job more pleasant, having someone to talk with. But Eric Williams was a network man. He had a big career ahead. It was 1930 and, for a young engineer, network radio was exciting.

And yet, Williams had to admit, he was just a small fry in a big operation like CBS. Most of the big stuff was in New York. And here he was, in Chicago, spending every morning in a church! If they wanted him to be the engineer for one of those big New York shows, like with Jack Benny or Rudy Vallee, now that was big time. But no, they sent him to do *sermons*. Where was his career headed? His life? Hmm, maybe nowhere fast!

Did anybody else ever feel that way? Sometimes Paul Rader talked about letters he got, letters that sounded like that. People looking for meaning, for something to fill the emptiness. Well, Williams could grant why they might tune in *The Breakfast Brigade*. If you listened long enough, that gospel stuff made some sense, in a certain kind of way. But of course, he was just the engineer. Being paid to do a job. He couldn't listen. Could he?

One day Clarence Jones came by. Nothing unusual in that. He said hello most every day. They often talked about radio. Jones had been there in 1922, playing in the brass quartet that day Paul Rader first broadcast from the roof of Chicago City Hall. Williams enjoyed that story, how the engineer cut a hole in the wall and told the quartet to play into a telephone. Radio had come a long way since then, and Jones was always saying how exciting it was for the gospel. But today Williams was ready to ask a few questions of his own. Jones sensed the engineer had something on his mind, and he seemed to know just the right answers. Day after day Williams had been broadcasting the preaching of Paul Rader, about repenting sin, trusting the Lord. At last he started to listen. And now it all clicked! Now he saw the need, saw it clearly. He and Jones talked together some more. Then at Jones's suggestion, the two men bowed their heads and began to pray.

A Hand on Their Shoulders

In the weeks that followed, Williams and Jones often talked excitedly together about using the "miracle means" of radio—as Paul Rader liked to say—to spread abroad the "Old Time Power" of the gospel. Then Jones began talking about some plans of his. Was Williams interested? Would he like to hear about them?

It went back to 1921. That's the year Jones met Paul Rader. Jones was a student then at Moody Bible Institute and often attended Moody Memorial Church where Rader preached. A year later, when Rader left Moody Church to found the Chicago Gospel Tabernacle, Jones was among a group of young men who joined the staff. And was it exciting! Rader was international president of the Christian and Missionary Alliance. His team was often on the road, doing the work of revivals and crusades and evangelistic campaigns. And at the church, Jones had a special burden for boys and girls. He had helped begin an "AWANA" youth program (the letters were from 2 Tim. 2:15 and stood for "Approved Workmen Are Not Ashamed") that was now spreading to other churches. But always, Jones had a vision for radio. God had allowed him to do many things, to make mistakes, to improvise, to learn by trial and error. Now Jones understood that training was for a purpose.

Two years ago, Jones explained to Williams, in 1928, he had gone to South America. Few radio stations existed there, so a strong signal might be heard across the continent. He began to scout for locations. Then last year, in the providence of God, he met a young evangelist traveling through Chicago. Reuben Larson had just come from a church conference in Duluth. One of the speakers was R. R. Brown, the famous radio preacher, who issued a ringing challenge to claim the airwaves for Christ. Larson was deeply moved. He told the Lord he would take the challenge if the chance ever came. Then he met Clarence Jones, and the two men quickly sensed the hand of the Lord upon their shoulders.

Now Larson was in Quito, Ecuador. He had been chasing one government official after another, asking for a radio license. They didn't quite know what to do. It would be the first radio station in the entire country—not to mention the first international evangelical radio station in the world. After months of inquiries, letters, and meetings, on August 15, 1930, the government at last granted the license. The official call letters were HCJB, "Heralding Christ Jesus' Blessings." Jones was preparing soon to leave the Chicago Gospel Tabernacle and join his friend in Ecuador. There was just one hitch. They had no transmitter. And they needed a radio engineer who could design and build one. Jones finished his story, and for a moment there was silence. Then there was prayer. Because Eric Williams, too, sensed the hand of God upon his shoulder.

Highways in the Skyways

On faith, Clarence Jones left a fruitful ministry with Paul Rader and the Chicago Gospel Tabernacle. On faith, Reuben Larson had lived two years already on the foreign field of Ecuador. And on faith, Eric Williams had quit a promising position at the CBS radio network, leaving the bright lights of the Windy City for the dark shadows of the Andes. But as Jones liked to say, they were "building highways in the skyways for the coming of the King." And too, they could be "confident of this very thing, that he who hath begun a good work in you will perform it until the day of Jesus Christ" (Phil. 1:6).

Yet folks back home were hard hit by the depression and contributions were scarce. Certainly, they could do nothing on the scale of Radio Vatican, which earlier that year, on February 22, 1931, had signed on the air as the first international religious station in the world. The Roman Catholic Church provided the funds, hiring the famous inventor of wireless radio, Guglielmo Marconi himself, to supervise construction of the 10,000-watt transmitter. Modern studios were now beaming religious services across Europe, direct from the great papal seat of Vatican City.

"The Voice of the Andes," however, was only a converted sheep shed on the outskirts of Quito, with a patched-up, jerry-built 250-watt transmitter.

But, at last, all was ready. The first broadcast, on Christmas Day 1931, lasted only two hours. Few people in Spanish-speaking Ecuador had radio sets. Yet the letters started coming. The gospel was getting through. Listeners were finding Christ. The broadcast schedule expanded. In its second year, the station added programs in the indigenous Quechua tribal language. In 1935 the HCJB signal was boosted to cover neighboring countries. Requests came from across the Andes for Bibles, for literature, for missionaries and churches, for pastoral training and medical services. A new transmitter in 1940 boosted "The Voice of the Andes" to a power of 10,000 watts, literally enough to be heard around the world.

Thank Him for the Answer

He was "Second Mate Bobbie." And with a thrill, he waited for the blast of the bosun's whistle, for the clang of eight bells, for the pipe organ to play. As a member of the crew of the Good Ship Grace, and baritone of the quartet, the music was his cue to sing, "I've anchored my soul in the Haven of Rest . . ." Then over the organ, a friendly voice came on the air, "Ahoy, there, shipmate! Eight bells and all's well." It was time again for *Haven of Rest*, heard each day at this hour, "coming to you from the harbor called Haven of Rest in Hollywood, California."

For Robert Bowman, the *Haven of Rest* ministry was as much a blessing to him as to the audience. As baritone soloist for the broadcast, he often received letters from listeners whose hearts were touched by his music. But most of all he was blessed by the many letters from those who had trusted Christ through the broadcast.

115

Then too, it was a blessing to work for Paul Myers, or "First Mate Bob" as he called himself on the air.

Myers knew how to reach his listeners, to reach them deep down, because that's where Jesus had reached him. Each broadcast began with eight bells for a reason. For it was the clanging of just such a bell that woke him from a drunken stupor one foggy morning in February 1934 as he lay by the San Diego harbor. Few people remembered it now, but "First Mate Bob" had once been a Hollywood celebrity. Back then, Myers led his own radio and motion picture orchestra. They called themselves the "Happy-Go-Luckies" and worked for Hal Roach Studios, one of the biggest movie studios of the day.

But life as a Hollywood musician was fast and fancy. Paul Myers reached the top—and alcohol plunged him just as quickly to the bottom. Until one cold and bitter dawn he was roused by the lonely clanging of a bell sounding out across the harbor. He struggled to his feet and realized it was Sunday morning. Church would begin soon, he thought. Perhaps it wasn't too late! With as much speed as he could muster, Myers hurried downtown to a nearby church and slipped into a pew just as the service was starting. Maybe someone would shake his hand, give a word of welcome, offer a ray of hope. But no one spoke to him, not even the minister. Disappointed, he staggered back to his cheap hotel room, and beside the bed he noticed an open Gideon Bible. He started to read.

Later that day, Myers walked into a telegraph office and sent a wire home. The simple message read, "Thank Him for the answer," but it was enough. Because for twelve years, Thelma Myers had prayed faithfully for her husband. Now he was coming home and, just thirty days later in March 1934, he was going back into the radio business. But this time as "First Mate Bob," inviting all who would listen to "anchor your soul in the Haven of Rest."

Robert Bowman had signed aboard the Good Ship Grace that same year, 1934, and in twelve years as Second Mate Bobbie he had seen *Haven of Rest* grow from a single local station to a daily slot on the Mutual West Coast Network. And once each week, the broadcast was aired nationwide.

Over the years he had seen thousands respond to the gospel, and in time a new burden gripped his heart. Around the globe a great war was raging. Each day the news reports told of distant, dying lands. If radio could reach so many in America, imagine what it could do to spread the gospel in other nations of the world!

He thought again of that vision, that day in 1945, as he stood quietly beside the docks of San Francisco, wrapping his overcoat tightly against the chill sea air. The war was over; the men were coming home. And now he was listening for the clang of a different bell. Not the Good Ship Grace, but the *Bon Homme Richard*, a U.S. Navy aircraft carrier of the 38th Task Force Fleet. Aboard was a young warrant officer, John Broger, an old classmate from their days together at Southern California Bible College. One day in 1938, when Broger was working in commercial radio, he came to Bowman with an idea to inspire Christian youth through a radio drama based on the heroic lives of missionaries past and present.

A fast friendship developed between the two men, and they met often to dream and talk together about the future. Sometimes they would go with their wives to the little restaurants in Los Angeles' Chinatown, and this turned their talk in a new direction. With the encouragement of Paul Myers, their thoughts turned to building radio stations in China to proclaim the gospel across the Orient. The bombs of Pearl Harbor interrupted their plans. But whenever the *Bon Homme Richard* was in home port, the two men talked and planned and prayed.

If anything, the war had fired John Broger with an even deeper devotion to overseas radio evangelism. His ship, the *Bon Homme Richard*, was the only carrier in the 38th Fleet equipped for night action. He often stood at his post upon the superstructure, scanning the inky blackness, listening for the drone of the fighter planes and torpedo bombers returning from action. Often the ship was swathed in banks of dense rolling fog, the flight deck lashed by screaming squalls that tossed the great carrier like a nutshell. The

117

pilots couldn't see the ship, and the crew couldn't see the planes. And there was nothing, nothing to guide seven tons of men and metal, hurtling at a hundred miles per hour toward a tiny wave-tossed speck in the ocean vastness, but radio.

They were flying blind, unable to see in the fog and storm, trusting entirely on the words in their headphones. And as each pilot dropped his landing gear and tail hook, as the landing signal officer gave the "cut" signal, as each plane jerked to a jarring halt on the flight deck, Broger whispered to himself, "I will guide thee with mine eye" (Ps. 32:8). Radio had brought them home out of the darkness.

Slow Boat to China

"Arrived Shanghai safely. Lining up appointments. Pray. John." It was a big day at the Far East Broadcasting Company when the telegram from John Broger arrived. It seemed the Lord was at last on the move! Just four months ago, in December 1945, Broger had received his discharge from the navy. Within days he and Robert Bowman, joined by Los Angeles pastor William Roberts, had pooled their resources—exactly $1,000. By December 20, the corporation papers were completed and FEBC was in business! And now Broger was in China, scouting locations for a radio station to proclaim the gospel across the war-torn reaches of East Asia.

But if the telegram was welcome news, Bowman and Roberts were sobered by the hard work behind them and the task still ahead. Paul Myers had graciously matched their first $1,000 and circulated a letter on behalf of FEBC to the large *Haven of Rest* mailing list. And because Bowman was recognized nationwide for his radio ministry, and Roberts was well known around Los Angeles, the two men were able to raise another $10,000 by March.

Yet ten times that amount, at least, would be needed to build a radio station in China. Bowman was preparing soon to leave First Mate Bob and the Good Ship Grace, to speak full time and raise funds for FEBC at church meetings and Bible conferences while tending the ministry office. And Broger, just three months after returning home from the war, had shipped out again to Shanghai on a salary of fifty dollars a week—after turning down an executive position with a leading glassware concern that promised a secure and prosperous future for his young family.

As the telegrams kept coming from Shanghai, however, Bowman and Roberts wondered if their fledgling ministry was on the right track. The Nationalist Chinese government of Chiang Kai-shek was locked in a rising civil war with communist insurgents led by Mao Tse-tung. The nationalist grip on the reins of government was often uncertain, and Broger was bounced from one office to another. Mostly the government feared that granting a radio franchise to FEBC, as a foreign concern, would weaken its position in denying franchises to communist groups. The nationalists would only make a "verbal" offer that an application "might" be considered—and only for 500 watts of power, a signal so weak as to be useless.

License for Unlimited Power

So after six months of negotiation, Broger boarded a Chinese tramp freighter bound for the Philippines. From Manila he hoped to catch a ship for home. Yet he arrived to find the country celebrating its second day of national independence. Fascinated, he decided to stay and investigate prospects for broadcasting from the Philippines. And with God's help, things started falling into place. Broger was befriended by a local attorney and newspaper publisher who introduced him to top officials of the new Filipino government. When he filed a station application with the Radio Department, leaving blank the signal strength (since he had no idea what to request), the commissioner wrote in, "Unlimited Power." And for a station site, two Christian businessmen offered to sell an ideal property near Manila at 60 percent below market value.

Broger plunked down the last $50 in his pocket to bind the option. Then Bowman wired $5,000 to secure the land. That left a balance of $15,000. To be paid in twenty-one days! Since the fledgling ministry didn't have money, the three partners made two decisions. First, once Broger got home to Los Angeles, they would spend a week together in prayer. And second, they would not borrow the funds. If this was a work of God, he would send the money in.

Their closing day of prayer was November 28, Thanksgiving Day. The payment for the Manila property was due December 1 and they were still $4,000 short. There was no mail on the holiday, so on Friday the three men went down to the post office. Not a single letter was in their box!

They turned to leave, but a mail clerk called out to them from the window. He said there was a package for them in the office. But when they went back inside, they found it was not a package.

Instead, they had received more mail than their post office box could hold. There were so many letters, the clerk had to bundle them all together! Gifts totaled $6,062, including $5,000 from a Chicago businessman they had never met and whose name they did not know. In a letter the man explained how the Holy Spirit had spoken to his heart one day at the office. At once he instructed his secretary, "Send a check for $5,000 to those young men out in California who have a vision for building a missionary radio station in the Orient."

From then on, the staff of Far East Broadcasting experienced one miracle after another. They had to! Their radio franchise was good only if FEBC was on the air by 8 P.M., April 14, 1948. Only sixteen months away! Within four months, however, the first FEBC missionary was on the field to clear the station site and put up staff housing. Prices for supplies were sky high, and communist guerillas often raided the district. Yet the authorities gave FEBC permission to purchase building materials on a priority basis. A well was dug by a Christian man dying of tuberculosis who wanted to do something lasting for the Lord. Cargo space was booked on faith to ship the transmitter from California, and God sent the $10,180 needed to make the sailing date. And when a typhoon halted work at the station site, the government granted a fifty-day extension.

But this time, FEBC *had* to begin broadcasting by 8 P.M., June 4, 1948, or the station would be deemed unable to perform. This time there would be no more extensions.

With Broger now in Manila to supervise operations, the eighteen-member staff set to work fourteen hours a day. Seven used Quonset huts were found at a bargain to house the men and their families. Telephone poles were obtained from the U.S. Navy, which gave them away to get them off their lot.

Then it happened. Three days before the deadline, when Broger had hoped the transmitter would be wired and ready for testing, a circuit went wrong. The equipment had to be repaired and rewired. The staff were frantic. Wires were hastily strung, then left in dense tangles on the floor. Lines from the power plant were run along makeshift crosspoles. Wives prayed as their husbands laid the high-voltage cable, often standing ankle deep in water left by the typhoon rains. Much was accomplished, but as Broger knew, much remained to be done. How could they possibly make it? If only they could have just a few more days.

All Hail the Power

On the morning of June 4, the day of the deadline, Broger drove into Manila. Over the past year he'd become a familiar face at many of the government offices. He was confident that, once the authorities saw how FEBC was so nearly ready, they would certainly grant a brief extension. He arrived in the city, hopes high, looking for the Lord to go before him. He sought for a door—but ran into a wall! Officials were away from the office, were in appointments, were hesitant to act alone. The more Broger tried, the more sure he became that no extension would be granted.

He decided to call "Christian Radio City" and pass on the news. The telephone lines were dead! Broger looked at his watch. It was past five. They had to be on the air by eight, in less than three hours! If he didn't start back now, he might not make it! The city roads were poor and streets were snarled about every other block. He raced from one traffic jam to another, dodged carts and wagons as he cut across narrow back alleys. At last, in a cloud of flying dust, Broger's car slid to a screeching stop outside the FEBC transmitter building. It was just before 6 P.M., only two hours to go before the deadline.

"No extra time granted! We've got to get her fired up now!" Broger yelled out to the men. "But we haven't even tested it once," protested the station engineer. "We'll test it on the air!" Broger shot back, running over to the console to grab a few pages of programming he had scribbled down. He shouted to start the power plant, to turn on the transmitter, to get ready to go on the air. Then, as a cautious grin appeared upon the sweating face of the engineer, Broger watched the panel as the needles on numerous dials started to swing into position! Frantically Broger called in the staff. As one, they bowed their heads to pray, to thank God for his miraculous help, to seek his blessing as they prepared to throw the master switch.

When the prayer was over, Broger and the staff looked up. It was almost 6 P.M. Just a few seconds before the hour. They watched as the seconds ticked down, transfixed, American and Filipino standing together, united in tears of thanksgiving and joy. At the stroke of six, the switch was thrown. Amid the tangle of wires and equipment, the staff raised their voices toward the sky. And across the airwaves of the great Pacific rang out the words of a glorious song: "Let every kindred, every tribe, on this terrestrial ball, to him all majesty ascribe, and crown him Lord of all!"

Then with a flick of his finger, the engineer motioned to Broger. He was on the air. "Ladies and gentlemen," he began, "this is the initial broadcast of KZAS [changed shortly after to DZAS], the new Call of the Orient station, located in Manila, Philippines. At this hour of 6:00 P.M., on June 4, 1948, the Far East Broadcasting Company lays before you the foundation for that which we believe to be the challenge of this generation—the challenge to do a work for God, the challenge of faith!"

Two hours later, the 1000-watt transmitter suddenly went dead, its circuits overloaded, the equipment automatically shut down. KZAS was off the air. Yet Broger wasn't too worried. The transmitter could be checked in the coming weeks as the station maintained a limited broadcast schedule. But on this day, when there was nothing left to do but throw the switch on faith, God allowed the transmitter to work just long enough. They had shown the proof of performance the government required. The radio franchise was safe. The Call of the Orient was secured.

The Spanish Connection

Paul Freed never forgot that muggy day in 1948 as he got off the train in Barcelona. As he sauntered about the old Moorish station, the summer heat oppressed body and spirit. What was he doing here? Freed had no idea! He had no interest in Spain, would rather have gone almost anywhere else in the world. Palestine and Syria, the exciting lands of his missionary childhood, were more to his liking. He knew no Spanish, had no particular concern for the Spanish people. But he had made a promise.

Never mind that Freed was thirty years old, married, supposedly settled. And that he already had a fruitful ministry as the local Youth for Christ director in Greensboro, North Carolina. When YFC founder Torrey Johnson had told him, "Paul, I believe God would have you go to Europe," he was soon on his way!

They sent him to a YFC missions conference in Switzerland, to hear men from across Europe present the needs of the continent. But two delegates made a special impression on his heart. They told of Spain, of believers relentlessly persecuted by the Catholic traditionalist regime of dictator Francisco Franco. In a land of thirty million people, only a handful of evangelical churches met openly. Most believers met secretly in their homes. The two missionaries pleaded for help and, reluctantly, Freed told them he would come for a few days after the conference and preach.

But in those days he saw a land and a people that captured his heart. He warmed to their courtesy, dignity, and friendly curiosity. Most of all, wherever he visited, he was blessed by the sturdy faith of the Spanish believers. In a tiny upper room church one day, Freed cast aside his sermon notes as a great lump rose in his throat. "You know God in a way I do not know him," he said through the interpreter. "Would you please let me sit at your feet? I want to hear something from you." The believers looked at each other in surprise for a moment; then an old gentleman came forward. "If there is one thing that is true in our lives," he explained, "it is that Jesus Christ means more than anything else to us."

From then on, Freed knew his burden was to multiply the blessings of Spanish Christians so that they might reach their own people with the gospel. In 1949, with a vision that had grown beyond the bounds of Greensboro, he left the secure salary of a local Youth for Christ director and began speaking in churches about the plight of Spanish believers. He began a modest construction business, building trailers and homes, and putting every extra cent into "the work." Then in 1951 he returned to Spain for an investigative trip, accompanied by his wife Betty Jane and another friend in the ministry, now with a conviction that gospel radio could be the means to reach Spain for Christ.

Beneath the Pine Grove

But no station sites were available. And the Franco government, which kept a tight rein over the media, was no friend of the evangelical church. Then Freed's interpreter made a suggestion. "You ought to go to Tangier. That's the best place for broadcasting." Tangier, in Morocco? Yes, it was an ideal location. The North African city was only twenty-six miles from the coast of Spain, across the narrow Strait of Gibraltar. And its status as a "free" port under international jurisdiction offered a unique opportunity to build a station. Yet Freed was at first reluctant. God had led him to Spain, *not* Tangier! Why would God move him, now, to Africa?

Then an old Spanish friend approached him with some advice. The man told him of two Spanish Christians in Tangier who had long prayed about a radio ministry for their country. "Why not let me take you to them, so you can at least talk?" So one morning they all took the ferry to Tangier, there to meet the two Spaniards. And all day long, the group of six spoke excitedly together about radio. That night at sunset, from the mountains overlooking the Strait of Gibraltar, they could see Spain. They had brought a picnic dinner to a fragrant pine grove outside Tangier, on the site of an old abandoned mission school. As they dreamed of the gospel going out across the waters, a desire also welled within them to give the old mission school new life as the site of their visionary station. Together in the gathering darkness, beneath the pine grove, they knelt to pray.

Next day, Freed inquired after the man who owned the school property. The search brought him to a tiny cottage. There he found a retired English missionary, eighty years old, who had given his life to the people of Tangier. As Freed explained his dream of reaching Spain by radio, the old missionary quickly caught the vision. Boldly, Freed asked if the man would pray about giving the property for a station site. And when the two got up off their knees, the gentleman declared, "Young man, if you can give your life for missions, the least I can do is give my property!"

From that moment, Freed knew radio was his ministry and Tangier was the address. The mission school property was offered to him for $15,000, a fraction of its value. To raise the funds, he returned to America and embarked with his wife and two infant children on a grueling deputation trip of 11,000 miles. His film footage of Spanish believers was turned into *Banderilla*, voted evangelical film of the year for 1952. Church showings around the country raised more than $100,000—enough so that on February 22, 1954, the "Voice of Tangier" was on the air!

Response to the radio outreach was beyond anything Freed had expected. Within five years, the original 2500 watts of transmitter power had been boosted nearly twenty times. Programs were being broadcast not only to Spain, but in more than thirty languages across all of Europe and North Africa, even piercing the Iron Curtain into captive nations of the communist East.

Many people had helped to make this growing outreach a reality. His father, Ralph Freed, had relinquished a new appointment as president of Canadian Bible Institute to join Paul in the work of missionary radio. And Ben Armstrong, his brother-in-law, had resigned a prosperous New Jersey pastorate to become director of home operations. Under the leadership of these three men, and with a staff of more than thirty missionaries, the Voice of Tangier had reached a new peak of effectiveness for the gospel.

Then in April 1959, the word came. In eight months it would all come to an abrupt and final end!

By Way of Monte Carlo

In the upheaval that followed the Second World War, Tangier had been declared a "free" city under international jurisdiction. Its status, along with its proximity to Spain, made the North African city an ideal base for the radio vision of Paul Freed. Yet the political winds were blowing in a new direction. The great European powers were exhausted by war, and the peoples of Africa clamored for an end to their colonial rule. Morocco gained its independence in 1959 and the city of Tangier was brought under its control. A new government was formed—and the authorities served notice that all radio was to be nationalized. The Voice of Tangier must be closed no later than December 31, 1959.

So Freed packed his bags—not to give up and go home, but to search out a new site for the radio ministry. With the trouble and turmoil in North Africa, he set his sights on Europe. In capital after capital, however, he found that, unlike in the United States, governments were opposed to private control of radio. As the

December deadline drew near to close the Voice of Tangier, Freed was quickly running out of options.

But he had a friend. And if this contact was the answer, then Freed marveled that it should have started with an offhand joke. Two years ago, in 1957, he was planning a trip to the United States. After praying with his mother about the journey, he quipped, "Maybe I'll go back to Greensboro by way of Monte Carlo." It was a joke, a reference to the capital of the tiny Mediterranean principality of Monaco, known the world over as a sumptuous gambling mecca for the international jet set. It was the most unlikely spot in all Europe for a missionary! And on the map, it was certainly out of his way. But Mother took it seriously. "Paul, boy," she said, "I think you should go to Monte Carlo. I think God is really in this." And sure enough, he went!

There he met the manager of Radio Monte Carlo, the government-owned agency that controlled broadcasting rights in the principality. And the manager had a problem. High above Monte Carlo, perched atop the great edifice of Mount Agel, was a massive stone structure. Nearly twenty years before, when Adolf Hitler had conquered the continent, he had chosen this site for a special purpose. Monaco was ideally situated to reach the airwaves of Europe, Asia, North Africa, and the Middle East. So here the German dictator constructed an incredible bombproof radio station to fill the world with Nazi hate.

But the war ended in defeat, the Nazi voice was stilled before the transmitters could be installed—and Radio Monte Carlo was stuck with an empty and unequipped facility, far too large for the needs of the tiny principality. Over the next two years, as he left Tangier for a time to pursue a doctorate in education in the United States, Freed gave some thought to adding a second station. Occasionally he corresponded with his friend about using the Monte Carlo site, just to keep in touch. But nothing ever came of it. His studies at New York University took most of his time. And things in Tangier were going fine.

Everything in Advance

Then came the closure decree from the Moroccan authorities. And though the announcement hit the staff like a bombshell, all were strangely sure the Lord would work something out. Within twenty-four hours, Freed was on a flight from New York to Monte Carlo. He had no idea what kind of reception awaited him. After all, for two years they had only exchanged occasional, noncommittal letters. But in the moment of crisis, he found the managers of Radio Monte Carlo now ready to discuss a contract!

In the months that followed, Freed explored other European sites. Yet he was more certain than ever that Monte Carlo was the only real possibility. Negotiations moved solidly ahead, but the terms were steep. The total cost of the installation—half a million dollars—had to be paid in advance. However, the sum could be broken into six payments. The first would be due when the contract was approved, and the remaining five paid out over the ensuing year. In all, six payments of $83,000 each!

To Paul Freed, even that partial sum sounded far beyond his grasp! But his friend at Radio Monte Carlo said the agency's board of directors would give him only one shot at an agreement, take it or leave it. No more negotiation. There was nothing left for Freed to do but either back out, or sign the contract on naked faith. God had set before him an open door, and Freed knew with all his heart that no man could shut it. So he signed. And somehow, each payment was made on time—once when a morning surge in the international exchange value of the dollar was just enough to cover a shortage on the day payment was due!

Fittingly, Charles Fuller's *Old-Fashioned Revival Hour* was the first program ever broadcast—on Sunday, October 16, 1960—by the newly named Trans World Radio. At the appointed hour, Paul Freed switched on his shortwave and tuned the dial. Huddled around the set with him in Monte Carlo were his wife and father, sister and brother-in-law. Every one of them had given their lives for this moment. An expectant hush filled the room, broken only by the crackle of the radio. Then the static faded. And across the air, via 100,000 watts of power, came the warm, familiar voice of Charles Fuller—as clearly as if he were there in person!

The tears of joy, sown that day by the five who gathered beside the little radio set, have since reaped a harvest far beyond the meager borders of Monaco. Today the Mount Agel station broadcasts the gospel via five powerful transmitters with a combined power of 2.7 million watts. And the work is now joined by seven more Trans World stations, located strategically across the globe, able to reach 80 percent of the world's population with gospel programs in one hundred languages.

Nor is Trans World Radio alone. The work begun in 1931 by Clarence Jones and Reuben Larson in a converted sheep shed has expanded into a global outreach. HCJB World Radio's Ecuador transmitter now beams shortwave programs in forty languages and dialects to six continents, while native language gospel radio and television programs are produced for distribution to local broadcast partners around the world. And the ministry of Far East Broadcasting today encompasses nearly thirty stations, bringing the gospel to Asia, India, Australia, China, the former Soviet bloc, and Latin America in scores of languages and dialects.

The God Who Came in from the Cold

Paul Freed walked into the office of the director general. Seven vinyl chairs had been arranged around a small coffee table. Upon the table was a neat stack of papers. He took a seat, near the window where an old air conditioner was laboring to relieve the August heat outside. The conversation, carried on through an interpreter, was pleasant and personable. Then with a smile and a flourish, he signed the contracts set before him. After that, he filled in the date, August 20, 1992.

And with that, it was now official. Trans World Radio now had the eighth transmitter site in its global gospel network. Yet Freed's thoughts wandered to his first site, the massive station in Monte

Carlo built by Adolf Hitler as an instrument of slavery and dictatorship. Each day on the air reminded him of the psalmist's prophecy, "Surely the wrath of man shall praise thee" (Ps. 76:10). Now the verse came to mind again. The contract papers, scattered upon the coffee table, were proof that the old prophecy had lost none of its power.

The new site was not built by Hitler. But two years ago, Radio Tirana was the most powerful communist propaganda station in all of Europe. Two transmitters with a combined power of 1,000,000 watts beamed forth the gospel to the only officially atheist society in the world. Though Albania was among the smallest nations of the globe, it was by far the most rigidly Marxist regime on earth. God was declared nonexistent. All religions were outlawed. Worship and prayer were punishable by death. And under the iron rule of dictator Enver Hoxha, Radio Tirana was built to proclaim the Revolution. But then the dictator died. Five years later, in 1990, his successors were deposed as another revolution swept across Eastern Europe. Communism was overthrown and freedom of religion was restored.

When Freed first saw Radio Tirana, he could not believe his eyes. The dictator had spared nothing. The mass of antenna systems was tremendous. Five sets of towers pointed to all the directions of Europe, while an array of eight towers pointed toward Russia. The powerful signal afforded an absolutely clear frequency with no interference. As he stood looking up at the arrays, he saw in his mind how the signal was even now beaming programs right through Yugoslavia to Romania and Hungary, and through Czechoslovakia into Ukraine and Russia beyond.

Now those same towers were set to send forth the glorious gospel of Jesus Christ. The first Trans World Radio broadcast was set for October 1, 1992. As Freed gathered up the contracts, then shook hands with the director general of the Albanian media authority, he again marveled how God had used the wrath of men to praise him. "Ye thought evil against me; but God meant it unto good, to bring to pass, as it is this day, to save much people alive" (Gen. 50:20).

A Photo History
of Christian Broadcasting

Calvary Episcopal Church was the site of the first religious broadcast, aired over KDKA/Pittsburgh on January 2, 1921. The broadcast, a Sunday vespers service, originated from the chapel shown above.

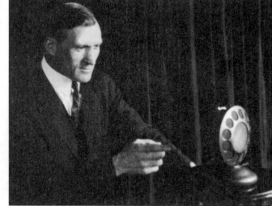

Paul Rader (left) began the first radio ministry in 1922, while R. R. Brown (right) started the first "radio church" in 1923, mobilizing listeners for prayer and charitable works as members of the World Radio Congregation.

When the government began to regulate the airwaves in 1927, stations such as KFSG (top) and WMBI (bottom) had to install professional equipment. Most religious stations could not afford to comply and went out of business.

The rise of national radio networks gave an unprecedented opportunity for the gospel. Walter Maier (left) and Charles Fuller (right) began network programs in the 1930s that ultimately reached millions of listeners.

When networks stopped selling airtime to evangelicals, broadcasters such as William Ward Ayer, shown during an altar call at New York's Calvary Baptist Church that was carried live by radio, were in danger of being put off the air.

James DeForest Murch (left) and Eugene Bertermann (right) petitioned the National Association of Evangelicals to sponsor the formation of what would become NRB in 1944. Both men later served as NRB presidents.

Percy Crawford (left) was the first evangelical on network TV in 1949. Billy Graham began telecasting *Hour of Decision* in 1950, and his 1957 New York Crusade, shown here, was the first crusade to be nationally televised.

The first Christian television station, WYAH-TV in Portsmouth, Virginia, was begun by Pat Robertson and went on the air in 1961. By 1966 his *700 Club* telethon developed into the first Christian talk show ever attempted.

Two 1970s inventions vastly expanded gospel broadcasts. Videotape (top) allowed mass syndication of programs. Satellite transmission was first demonstrated at the 1971 NRB convention, shown here with Theodore Epp (bottom).

Pat Robertson's Christian Broadcasting Network was first in using satellite in 1977 (top). During the decade, entertaining religious programs such as the *Rex Humbard World Outreach Ministry* were popular in syndication (bottom).

President Gerald Ford's appearance at the 1976 NRB convention and subsequent meeting with religious broadcasters at the White House was a turning point in awakening evangelicals to their potential influence.

In 1976 NRB interviewed both presidential candidates, including Jimmy Carter, shown at top with (left to right) Ben Armstrong, Brandt Gustavson, and Jimmy Waters of the Southern Baptist Radio-TV Commission. When Carter spoke as president to the 1980 NRB convention (bottom), broadcasters applauded his faith but questioned his policies.

The 1980s brought explosive growth and national prominence for religious broadcasters. Presidents Ronald Reagan (left) and George Bush (right) were regular visitors to NRB conventions.

Gospel radio reached around the world through the pioneering missionary efforts of (left to right) Clarence Jones of HCJB Radio, Robert Bowman of the Far East Broadcasting Company, and Paul Freed of Trans World Radio.

B. Sam Hart

Benjamin Smith

Luis Palau

Paul Finkenbinder

Pioneers of ethnic religious broadcasting that assumed vital importance in the 1980s.

Paul Myers, *Haven of Rest*

M. R. DeHaan, *Radio Bible Class*

J. Vernon McGee, *Thru the Bible*

Theodore Epp, *Back to the Bible*

Pioneers who founded programs still popular today.

James Dobson,
Focus on the Family

Chuck Swindoll,
Insight for Living

Charles Stanley, *In Touch*

D. James Kennedy,
Truths That Transform

Some of today's top radio broadcasters.

Jerry Falwell,
Old Time Gospel Hour

Robert Schuller, *Hour of Power*

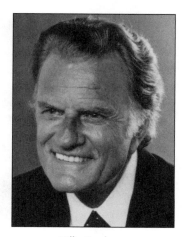

Billy Graham

Jack Van Impe,
Jack Van Impe Presents

Some of today's highest rated television broadcasters.

Under the leadership of Ben Armstrong (left), who retired as executive director in 1989, and now president E. Brandt Gustavson, NRB has implemented guidelines to ensure broadcasters' financial and ethical integrity.

Abe Van Der Puy, HCJB World Radio, (1975–78)

David Hofer, KRDU-AM/Dinuba, California, (1979–82)

Robert Cook, *The King's Hour,* (1985–88)

Jerry Rose, WCFC-TV/Chicago, (1988–91)

David Clark, KMC Media, (1991–94)

Robert Straton, Walter Bennett Communications, (1994–)

NRB chairmen since 1975.

7

THE PROMISE OF POWER

1978–1987

B en Armstrong could feel the electricity. Across the cavernous
ballroom of the Shoreham Americana Hotel, he could hear
the quiet motions of three thousand broadcasters and guests,
all silently joining hands to pray for the nation. And to pray for
the man who stood beside him on the platform. As Armstrong felt
the hand of the president of the United States reaching over to
clasp his own, he was jolted by a sudden electric sensation of an
even greater Hand reaching across the hush of the ballroom. In
his ten years as executive secretary of National Religious
Broadcasters, never had he experienced such a deep spiritual unity
among so many. That Sunday evening in Washington, February

22, 1976, was a moment he would never forget. The convention program called it "A Prayer for the Nation." But Armstrong sensed much more. This opening session of the NRB Bicentennial Convocation, held that year in conjunction with the National Association of Evangelicals, was the start of something that had been waiting to happen. You could just sense it!

For one thing, Armstrong noticed something he'd never seen at an NRB convention before. Network news cameras were popping up at panel sessions. Reporters were clamoring for credentials. The national media had "discovered" the seeming novelty of public figures who "got religion." The notion that athletes, entertainers, and executives might have evangelical convictions was a brand-new angle—now that nationally syndicated gospel television programs had brought them to public attention. Of course, broadcasters such as Rex Humbard and Oral Roberts were celebrities in their own right. But when convicted Watergate conspirator Charles Colson and pop singing star Pat Boone addressed an NRB session on morality in media, Armstrong couldn't believe how many camera crews were on hand to record the event.

The 1976 NRB Bicentennial Convocation also marked, Armstrong noted, the first time he had publicly shared his controversial conception of the "electric church," coining a phrase that would soon fuel a national debate. Yet to the NRB executive secretary, the most important "first" really occurred about a month before the main event.

Ties That Bind

His secretary said it was from Washington. Hmm, probably something about the convention next month. Maybe the hotel or the caterer. He casually picked up the phone. But in an instant his attention was riveted to the voice on the other end. It was the White House! Ordinary people didn't get calls from the White House, he thought to himself. Only astronauts and Super Bowl coaches got calls from the White House. But here was a top aide asking whether NRB might allow President Gerald Ford to address its upcoming convention. The aide apologized for the short notice. But could the association send an invitation and find a place on its program?

The next few minutes were a blur. Armstrong managed to stammer out his appreciation, assure the aide an invitation would be promptly sent, and hang up. Then as the NRB executive secretary recovered his breath, it all began to register. Each year, Armstrong knew, the president of the United States received thousands of invitations from all over the world. Only a handful could be accommodated. For the White House to call and ask for an invitation was almost more than he could fathom. True, President Ford had addressed the 1975 convention. But that was only after months of calls and courting and pulling strings. It was quite a coup then, and Armstrong could hardly expect to pull it off two years in a row. Now here was the White House calling *him!*

Yet broadcasters had been working for this payoff for twenty years. James Murch brought the NRB convention to Washington in 1956 so the young organization could cultivate a presence in the seat of national power. Now Armstrong was reaping the harvest, sown by years of quiet toil as broadcasters nurtured and tended friendships on Capitol Hill. Over the years Armstrong had often greeted Gerald Ford at the annual NRB Congressional Breakfast, first as a congressman from Michigan and then as Republican minority leader for the House of Representatives. Even during the national ordeal of Watergate, when he was elevated to vice president of the United States, Gerald Ford had attended the yearly NRB Congressional Breakfast.

Though the new president seldom spoke in public about his religious beliefs, he had readily professed to Armstrong a vital and long-standing born-again faith in Christ. He felt at home among evangelicals. His hometown, Grand Rapids, was a denominational headquarters and national center for learning and publishing in the Reformed evangelical tradition. His son Stephen Ford was preparing for the ministry at Gordon-Conwell College of Massachusetts, a leading evangelical institution headed by none other than Harold Ockenga—who was slated to be a principal speaker at the 1976 Convocation. And one of the president's closest boy-hood friends, and now a spiritual mentor, was a leading NRB member and prominent Christian filmmaker.

Awakening a New Awareness

When the day of the convention arrived, Armstrong was excited. The NRB and NAE staffs had been working on the event—promotion and registration, lodging and programs—for more than a year. Now delegates were streaming into the Shoreham Americana by the hundreds, buzzing with the news that Gerald Ford, the president of the United States, would address the night's opening session. As he watched the workers hang the presidential seal on the ballroom podium, saw the Secret Service agents with their radios going over the security arrangements, Armstrong knew something very special was afoot.

By 8:30 the delegates were assembled in the Grand Ballroom. The houselights were dimmed and a quiet and expectant hush settled over the convention. President Ford was accorded the seat of honor to the right of the podium, and Armstrong in turn was seated next to the president. The two men exchanged pleasantries, then fell silent as the session was called to order.

With the bond of Christian fellowship and shared experience that broadcasters enjoy, the evening swiftly evolved into a special event. Then at last, as the network cameras rolled and photographers jostled up front for a good position, evangelist Jess Moody stepped to the podium. He called for a special closing prayer for the president of the United States. And he asked the three thousand assembled delegates and guests to follow a custom of the church he pastored. "Just join hands with the person beside you," he said, reaching over to clasp the hand of the president beside him. Gerald Ford looked surprised for only a moment; then in a natural gesture of deep faith he bowed his head and firmly reached over to take the hand of Ben Armstrong. In that moment the NRB executive secretary sensed a surge of spiritual electricity, from the hand of the president through his own and out to thousands of hands joined across the immense ballroom.

Next day, newspapers across the country carried front-page photos of President Ford and Jess Moody with heads bowed and hands joined in prayer. To the media, such public piety from a president was certainly not politics as usual! Armstrong himself believed, as he wrote later, that "something new happened at our recent convention . . . a growing sense of commitment to bring our country back to God and to his leadership . . . to speak and act as the servants of the living God. By awakening a new awareness of our own strength and a new willingness to act, the Convocation marked a turning point for evangelicals.

"As we left Washington for our own broadcasting studios, offices, classrooms, and churches, we had a new commission to reclaim our nation for God and to rescue it from the erosion of secular humanism. There was a new willingness to leave our evangelical enclaves and become more spiritually alive and incisively active in this age and this society to which God has called us. After years of watching from the sidelines as America drifted away from the teachings of the Bible, evangelical Christians now were ready to give an affirmative, vigorous response to the call of God. In a sense, the Bicentennial Convocation charted the course for a whole new media strategy to share Jesus Christ. Washington, D.C., February 1976, promises to go down in history as the start of a new era in the role of American evangelicals."

Honesty about Religion

It was the second time in as many weeks he had been to the White House; indeed, the second time he had been seated next to the president in less than a month. That first meeting, September 16, Ben Armstrong had gone to the Oval Office as head of the NRB *World Religious News*, a service formed by the association in 1974 to provide religious broadcasters with new programming for their growing audiences. Armstrong was the staff producer of *World Religious News*, and he had gone to Washington with President Nathan Bailey of the National Association of Evangelicals and senior editor Arthur Matthews of *Christianity Today*. They had come to interview the president, to present him with fourteen questions of concern to evangelical Christians, so his answers could be shared with listeners and viewers of the nation's religious media. Later the session would be made into a half-hour documentary distributed to some 150 *World Religious News* subscribers, with transcripts released to more than four hundred religious and secular publications.

More importantly, Armstrong thought, the September 16 interview marked perhaps the first time in the modern era that a candidate for the presidency of the United States had been invited, candidly and directly, to share his personal relationship with Jesus Christ—not in a judgmental way, but allowing the candidate to freely describe his spiritual values and how they influenced his life and decisions. Armstrong had been heartened to hear President Ford reiterate his deep faith in God, and had likewise been gratified when the president cordially agreed to meet again with a larger NRB delegation two weeks later.

Now in his second White House meeting, on September 30, Armstrong was again seated next to the president, joined this time by thirty-four religious broadcasters from many of the largest Christian media organizations in the nation and the world. As they gathered about the massive oak conference table in the ornate Cabinet Room, the broadcasters queried President Ford on topics ranging from FCC regulations and the impact of foreign policy on overseas missions to the key social and economic issues that concerned their listeners. The session was enlivened by the president's confidential assertion that, unlike his election opponent, he had refused an interview to *Playboy* magazine—a decision that drew especial praise from Jerry Falwell, who later aired his disagreement with the Democratic candidate.

Armstrong, however, was careful to keep NRB neutral in the presidential race. In that spirit, *World Religious News* offered the Democratic nominee, Governor Jimmy Carter of Georgia, the chance to be interviewed with the same fourteen questions put earlier to President Ford. The NRB executive secretary knew many Christians were drawn by the Georgian's frank assertion of a born-again faith. While the president preferred the traditional reluctance to air religious views in public, Carter openly presented himself as a man of faith. Just as openly, he sought the votes of religious Americans. Pols and pundits remarked how the Georgia peanut farmer had put personal piety back on the political map. Until then, talk of a candidate's religion had been taboo—especially since 1960 when John F. Kennedy, a Roman Catholic, faced down critics who suggested his policy decisions could be swayed by the Pope.

Candidates of Commitment

When word came that candidate Carter would talk with *World Religious News*, Armstrong was gratified. Religious broadcasters were playing a key role in uniting evangelical Americans as a cohesive social force, providing a national Christian medium for news and information from a biblical perspective. Getting an interview with the Democratic nominee showed that, at the highest levels of national politics, the major parties saw the emergence of a new evangelical bloc. And it didn't hurt to have NRB members in the right places. Governor Carter, a Southern Baptist active in church circles, was a longtime friend of NRB board member Jimmy Waters, then chairman of the denomination's Radio-TV Commission and president of the Georgia Baptist Convention. With all that going for him, Armstrong quickly obtained an interview for October 14 during a Carter campaign stop in Indianapolis.

On the day of the interview, Armstrong and Waters were joined by NRB vice president E. Brandt Gustavson of Moody Radio Network and *World Religious News* correspondent Ken Gaydos of KGDN/Seattle. Because of the candidate's busy schedule, the *News* team moved quickly to its list of questions. In reply, Governor Carter firmly stated that "in his opinion" abortion and homosexuality were wrong because they violated biblical standards. He saw international communism as a threat to American security and especially deplored Soviet persecution of its five million Baptists. As for prayer in public schools and tuition tax credits for parents who send their children to Christian schools, the Georgian referred to his Southern Baptist heritage of strict separation between church and state.

Then the four NRB members listened as the Democratic nominee put aside his busy schedule and spoke freely for more than forty-five minutes about his faith in the Lord. The governor recalled how he had made a personal commitment to Jesus as a boy of eleven, how he had grown spiritually by daily Bible study and prayer, and how in the 1960s he had experienced his "deepest, most personal turning to Christ." Carter certainly knew how to touch the evangelical heart! Armstrong wondered how this difference might affect the outcome in what looked like a very close election. Yet he firmly believed and reported that both candidates were "men of Christian commitment. While they differed in their views . . . they had a common meeting ground at the foot of the Cross."

Thus, he predicted "the real winner in 1976 is the Christian community . . . [for] this campaign has made the secular media aware of the fifty to sixty million evangelicals, the hitherto silent core of Christianity in America." The electric church "is increasingly an acknowledged factor on the American scene," he declared, and religious broadcasters would continue in the future to inform "our viewers and listeners [who] want to know about the spiritual life of the candidates and how they relate their religious convictions to the key issues facing the nation."

Shaping Evangelical Opinion

As for media attention, Armstrong was right. Many credited the evangelical vote with making the difference as Carter edged Ford in a razor-thin victory. By 1978 the annual NRB convention was recognized by reporters as the premier gathering of evangelical leaders. Media representatives that year at the Washington Hilton Hotel ranged from the national broadcasting corporations of Sweden and Australia, to network correspondent Roger Mudd reporting on the "boom in born-again broadcasting." According to *Broadcasting* magazine, the NRB event drew an "army of reporters . . . [that] looked like a directory of the national and foreign press corps." An appearance by singer Anita Bryant, who had fought a "gay rights" law in her Florida county, was greeted by a candlelight march of homosexual activists around the convention hotel. Notorious pornographer Larry Flynt and former Black Panther Eldridge Cleaver, men who now claimed to be born again, both turned up to gain publicity for their causes.

But despite growing media awareness of an evangelical awakening, Christian broadcasters soon came to believe it *did* matter who was in the White House. The Carter administration endorsed the Equal Rights Amendment and tax-funded abortions. A White House Conference on Families shut out evangelicals, though a newcomer to religious radio, James Dobson of the *Focus on the Family* broadcast, authored a minority report. The president signed away the Panama Canal, recognized the Chinese communist regime of Mao Tse-tung, and offered arms concessions to the Soviet Union. Taxes were raised. New federal regulations tied business in knots. And the FCC proposed quotas for granting licenses to minority groups, plus a requirement that stations consult homosexuals about programming.

In 1978 came the one issue that, more than any other, galvanized the evangelical community into direct action. With the approval of President Carter, the Internal Revenue Service proposed a rule that *assumed* any private school "formed or substantially expanded at or about the time of public school desegregation in the community served by the school" was guilty of racial discrimination and must be stripped of its tax-exempt status unless the school could prove otherwise. Reaction to this attack was swift and intense. Christians nationwide arose with one voice, united in their zeal to preserve the right to give their children a biblical education without undue government interference.

Word quickly went out through a network of evangelical media that did not exist even five years before. Religious broadcasting had indeed come a long way since *The 700 Club* debuted in 1966 as the first Christian talk show on television. Now attorneys and activists were booked on the Robertson program or the popular *PTL Club* with Jim Bakker. Radio call-in programs, a phenomenon sweeping the secular media, likewise found a ready audience among evangelicals. Phone lines lit up as listeners nationwide dialed *Point of View* with Marlin Maddoux, *Talk Back* with Bob Larson, and *Open Line* on the Moody Radio Network. Like never before, religious broadcasters had become the agent in shaping an evangelical consensus.

Scrambled Eggs and Grits

Religious broadcasters hadn't been to the White House in four years. Much had changed. A new president, a new administration, a new party. And many new questions. At first the conversation had been jovial and relaxed, enjoyed over a hearty breakfast of scrambled eggs and grits. But now, across the great oval table of the Executive Dining Room, looks of disappointment and concern crossed the faces of many of the leading names in gospel radio and television. And they had come with such high hopes.

Only last night, January 21, President Carter had addressed a glorious session of the 1980 NRB convention. More than four thousand broadcasters and guests rose to their feet, greeting the president with a heartfelt standing ovation, a sincere outpouring of love for a fellow brother in Christ. For nearly five minutes, the raucous cheers and applause rang across the grand ballroom of the Washington Hilton Hotel. Carter was visibly moved and responded with a warm speech that showed a familiar command of the Bible, comparing the power and responsibilities of the presidency to those of gospel broadcasters. Then the president invited NRB leaders to join him and share their views at a private White House breakfast the next morning.

Of course, only now in an election year had Jimmy Carter made the first visit of his four-year term to an NRB convention. Concern over the liberal drift of his administration had led Ben Armstrong, several months before, to call a Washington "summit conference" of leading NRB members to consider a common agenda for boosting Christian involvement in the political process. The group included broadcasters Jerry Falwell, Pat Robertson, Jim Bakker, and Jimmy Swaggart, along with conservative strategists Pat Buchanan, Ed McAteer, John Conlan, and Gary Jarmin. That same year, 1979, Falwell launched the Moral Majority, destined to be the linchpin of grassroots activism in the coming decade. Robertson formed The Freedom Council, as McAteer established the Religious Roundtable, and Conlan the FaithAmerica Foundation.

Yet when President Carter came to the NRB convention, gospel broadcasters were glad to welcome him with open arms. They did not always agree with his policies, but they admired the way he upheld Christ in his personal life, attending church, teaching Sunday school, even sharing his faith with world leaders. And it was that spirit which brought an NRB delegation to the White House next morning for scrambled eggs and grits—a delegation led by NRB vice president Brandt Gustavson and joined by Jerry Falwell, Oral Roberts, Rex Humbard, Jim Bakker, James Kennedy, Jimmy Waters, and Jimmy Allen of the Southern Baptist Radio-TV Commission, Charles Stanley of the *In Touch* program, Tim LaHaye of *Family Life Seminars*, and Howard Jones of *Hour of Freedom*. Together they sincerely hoped, as they had first hoped during the election four years before, to find with the president of the United States "a common meeting ground at the foot of the Cross."

Faith without Works

As the broadcasters finished their breakfast, however, they could see more clearly than ever that President Carter drew a sharp line between his private conduct and public actions. They expected his usual objection to school prayer but were surprised by his unwillingness to hear their concerns about the proposed Equal Rights Amendment. They pointed out that today, January 22, marked seven years since the Supreme Court had legalized abortion in its *Roe v. Wade* decision. Across the street from the White House, on the Ellipse, tens of thousands of Christians were assembling for the annual March for Life. Did the president acknowledge any of their concerns? He offered only vague answers. When the delegation asked about the lack of evangelicals in his administration against scores of liberal appointments, President Carter was again non-committal.

Perhaps like no other event, the White House session pointed out two basic issues for broadcasters. Four years ago, Ben Armstrong had declared that, in using religious media, evangelicals "had a new commission to reclaim our nation for God and to rescue it from the erosion of secular humanism." But now it was clear that broadcasters first had a decision to make. What was most important in a political leader? His personal faith? Or his public actions? In President Carter they had a sincere brother of like faith, one who faithfully upheld his commitment in private but whose public leadership allowed the liberal agenda to prosper. Despite their respect for the president as a Christian, the evangelical broadcast community ultimately concluded that "faith without works is dead."

Faith is examined in private, but policies are public record. And that brought up a second issue. For sixty years, broadcasters had used the airwaves chiefly for *evangelism*. Now they faced something new. To keep Christians informed and active, they must begin to practice *journalism*, a discipline with new demands for handling information in a responsible manner. President Carter was at least right in saying the power to shape evangelical opinion gave broad-casters a great responsibility.

Between 1972 and 1982, the electric church exploded. More than a thousand organizations, a threefold increase over the ten years, were producing religious radio and television programs. Christian media reached virtually every major market in America as radio stations doubled during the decade from four hundred to nearly nine hundred, and television soared from twenty-five to seventy-nine. Together with three national Christian satellite TV networks formed in 1977–78, religious broadcasting reached a weekly audience variously estimated at between 15 and 130 million. Here indeed was the potential to mobilize a movement for God! How would broadcasters manage as *evangelists* in the traditional task of getting out the gospel, as well as in their newfound role as *journalists* in keeping the nation's Christians informed?

Call to the Faithful

April 29, 1980. Ben Armstrong marked it down. It was the first time that the "fourth network" of Christian media had worked together as one unit. More than 120 broadcast professionals from eight Christian television organizations had pooled their resources to cover Washington for Jesus, one of the most miraculous events he had ever witnessed. Eight live cameras were stationed around the Mall, while minicam crews moved through the crowd and a helicopter cameraman hovered overhead. Armstrong was asked to offer the closing prayer, and as he looked across the Mall over a vast sea of faces estimated at between a quarter and half a million, he knew this was history in the making.

According to broadcaster Bill Bright of Campus Crusade for Christ, Washington for Jesus was "the broadest representation of the body of Christ in the history of the church." Others said the event was the largest gathering ever held in the nation's capitol, larger than the Civil Rights marches and antiwar protests of the past two decades. The city had never seen anything like it! From sunrise until sundown the main order of business was prayer, not protest. Reporters looked for hidden political motives. And when John Giminez, the Virginia pastor who inspired the event, said God had merely given him a vision to pray for the nation, the secular media was incredulous.

Washington for Jesus also demonstrated, as Armstrong saw it, how the electric church had taken a leading role in mobilizing Christians to take back their country. Of the sixty speakers at the rally, most by far were radio or television broadcasters. Paul Crouch, Jim Bakker, Rex Humbard, D. James Kennedy, Charles Stanley, James Robison, Robert Schuller, Carl Richardson, Ben Haden, E. V. Hill, Lester Sumrall, and many more. Pat Robertson and Bill Bright were cochairmen of the event. And the massive outpouring of Christians on the Mall—who had come by plane, train, car, and more than eleven hundred buses from every state in the Union—was in no small part a testimony to the power of the electric church for calling the faithful to action.

That power was evident again a few months later, in August 1980, when religious broadcasters helped bring fifteen thousand pastors to Reunion Arena in Dallas for a National Affairs Briefing sponsored by the Religious Roundtable. The major presidential candidates had been invited to address the conference, and the Republican nominee, Ronald Reagan, agreed to attend. Over the past year, evangelical leaders had been getting to know the former California governor, even as they met with other prospective candidates. Gospel broadcasters first got to meet Ronald Reagan in July 1979, when Arizona congressman John Conlan—who was himself a former associate of Billy Graham and Bill Bright—organized a meeting at the Atlanta Omni Hotel with fifty broadcast and ministry executives.

From the beginning, broadcasters were impressed by Reagan's conservative views, sensitivity to evangelical concerns, and personal Christian testimony. Individual preachers developed close personal ties to the candidate, particularly Jerry Falwell, who was traveling in Taiwan when Reagan called him long-distance from the Republican National Convention in Detroit to ask his advice on a vice presidential nominee. (The Virginia evangelist suggested George Bush.) Falwell later arrived at the Detroit convention, where he was a factor in shaping the GOP platform and his Liberty Singers performed in prime time.

Now Falwell shared the platform again with Governor Reagan, appearing with him at the National Affairs Briefing in Dallas along with broadcasters James Robison, D. James Kennedy, and W. A. Criswell. For the 350 reporters on hand to cover the event, most of whom had never seen a pulpit-pounding preacher in person, the two-day conference was an eye-opener! While they never really understood the evangelical movement, the presence of Ronald Reagan got their attention. The role of religious broadcasters and "the Christian vote" became one of the hottest and most intensely debated stories of the 1980 campaign.

Throughout the many speeches and messages, candidate Reagan listened intently. Then striding to the podium, he put aside his prepared text for a moment and offered an impromptu declaration. "Now, I know this is a nonpartisan gathering, and so I know you can't endorse me," he told the Reunion Arena audience, "but I want you to know that I endorse *you* and what you are doing!" A thunderous ovation went up from the crowd, applause and cheers ringing with shouts of "Amen!" Then the GOP nominee rounded out his remarks by telling the assembled preachers and pastors, "I have found there is a new vitality in American politics. You are the reason. Religious America is awakening, perhaps just in time for our country's sake."

In September and October, Armstrong and NRB sponsored news conferences with independent presidential candidate John Anderson and with Governor Reagan so that representatives of the "fourth network" could air their questions on issues of evangelical concern. These sessions—the latter held at Liberty Baptist College before eight thousand cheering students and guests—were carried extensively on Christian radio and television, so that listeners and viewers could hear the candidates' answers without the distortion of the secular media. The Carter White House, however, stalled until the final weeks of the campaign. Finally, an aide admitted to Armstrong that the incumbent did not need to meet with the Christian media because he "had the evangelical vote sewed up."

Climate for Growth

When the votes were counted in November, though, it was clear the evangelical vote had made a massive switch to the Republican column. Christians had heard the candidates and preferred the promise of private faith translated into public action. Ronald Reagan was elected president of the United States. For eight years, the "Reagan Revolution" made conservative issues the dominant political agenda of the nation. In this climate, religious broadcasting continued to flourish as never before. During the Reagan presidency, the number of domestic Christian radio stations climbed to more than eleven hundred and television to more than three hundred, with more than eleven hundred religious organizations producing programs for broadcast.

Many of these broadcasts grew to national prominence and influence, including *Focus on the Family* with James Dobson, a professor of pediatrics who in 1977 felt led of God to do something to stop the unprecedented disintegration of the American family. Starting in a two-room suite in Arcadia, California, and a twenty-five-minute weekly radio program heard on just a few dozen regional stations, Dobson endured the scorn of liberal detractors, who decried his scriptural advice for marriage and child discipline as hopelessly outdated, to see *Focus on the Family* become the largest syndicated radio program in the history of religious broadcasting.

Not since the 1940s and the heyday of Walter Maier and Charles Fuller had America ever seen such a gospel radio phenomenon! Within fifteen years of its founding, *Focus on the Family* had become a national movement, saying to listeners "turn your hearts toward home" through broadcasts heard daily on more than four thousand stations worldwide. Today, with more than fifty ministries and twelve hundred employees headquartered in Colorado Springs, Colorado, *Focus on the Family* produces seven radio broadcasts, publishes eight magazines with a monthly circulation of nearly three million, coordinates a referral network of twelve hundred family counselors, and is a leading producer of Christian books, films, and videos.

Paced by the success of *Focus on the Family*, the 1980s saw a renaissance of gospel radio. After a generation of giving ground to television, broadcasters now rediscovered the power of radio, not only as a lower cost alternative to the visual media, but as a uniquely intimate way to reach new listeners. During the decade, gospel radio entered a new golden age with national audiences for such programs as *In Touch* with Charles Stanley, *Insight for Living* with Charles Swindoll, and *Truths That Transform* with D. James Kennedy.

On television, the Christian Broadcasting Network had become in the 1980s the third largest cable system in the nation, behind only the Cable News Network and ESPN, with annual revenues of $230 million and a monthly cumulative audience for *The 700 Club* of twenty-nine million. The Trinity Broadcasting Network had grown to become the world's largest producer and distributor of original Christian programming. And the PTL Television Network, along with the new ACTS satellite network of the Southern Baptist Radio and Television Commission, wasn't far behind.

More Voices for the Gospel

In the rising tide of gospel radio and television, urban and ethnic voices began to establish a dynamic presence of their own. And for Black broadcasters, with a long but little recognized heritage, 1978 was a signal year. Under the banner of the four-year-old NRB Ethnic Broadcasters Committee (now Black National Religious Broadcasters, or BNRB), Blacks in radio and television held their first "strategy conference" to at last become full partners in proclaiming the gospel over the airwaves.

In August 1978, evangelist B. Sam Hart, whose *Grand Old Gospel Hour* was syndicated on 130 outlets worldwide, launched WYIS/Philadelphia as the first Black American evangelical to own a radio station. A month later, WGPR-TV/Detroit went on the air with a religious format, the first Black-owned television station in the nation. And Cleophus Robinson, already seen in seventy-five cities, was in May 1978 the first Black preacher to telecast outside the continental United States when his gospel music and preaching program began airing in Puerto Rico and Hawaii.

Pastor Benjamin Smith, Sr., of Philadelphia's Deliverance Evangelistic Church became perhaps the first Black preacher with a regular program on satellite television when his *Time of Deliverance* was picked up in October 1978 by the PTL Television Network. Earlier that year, in April, evangelist Fred Price began telecasting *Ever Increasing Faith* on KTBN/Los Angeles, in what would soon become a national satellite outreach over the Trinity Broadcasting Network. And at the Christian Broadcasting Network, where the satellite space race had started a year earlier, folksy cohost Ben Kinchlow of *The 700 Club*—once a Malcolm X disciple who hated white people with a consuming rage—was fast becoming a favorite for audiences of all races.

These men were carrying on a long tradition that had begun with such early Black radio preachers as Clayton Russell, who went on the air in 1936 over KFOX/Los Angeles. In 1939, the "father" of Black gospel radio, Joe Bostick, launched *The Gospel Train* on WCNW/New York in a day when few stations were even aware of the music. The South's first Black radio preacher, Pastor William Holmes Borders, Sr., of Atlanta's Wheat Street Baptist Church, began broadcasting over WGST in 1943 with a program called *Seven Minutes at the Mike in the Deep South* that was carried around the globe during World War II over Armed Forces Radio.

Over the years and into the decade of the 1980s, Black religious broadcasters built regional and national audiences drawn to their dynamic biblical preaching, among them Howard Jones of *The Hour of Freedom*, Joseph "Preacher" Brown of *The Grace Memor-*

ial Hour, Clay Evans of *What a Fellowship Hour*, Bishop Smallwood Williams of *Man and a Message*, Anthony Evans of *The Urban Alternative*, Bishop Samuel Green, Jr., of the Church of God in Christ, and J. Morgan Hodges of the Ethnic Broadcasting Foundation, the nation's first broadcaster to operate a radio station from a correctional institution at the Lorton Reformatory in Virginia.

Another gospel voice from the cities of America, for the nation's booming Hispanic population, also took its place as a vital player in religious broadcasting. Pioneering programs often started as Latin American outreaches, then moved to the U.S. as the need grew for Spanish-language evangelism at home. *Un Mesaje a la Conciencia* with Paul "Hermano Pablo" Finkenbinder began during 1955 in El Salvador, and the *Cruzada* and *Responde* broadcasts of Luis Palau were first heard during 1964–65 in Argentina. Both are now aired across the United States, as well as around the Spanish-speaking world.

Under the auspices of NRB, the Hispanic National Religious Broadcasters (HNRB) was created in 1981. Membership quickly grew during the decade as both independent ministries and denominational broadcast departments began producing Hispanic programs for the U.S. market.

Signs on the Horizon

Despite the spectacular growth of religious broadcasting, there were some worrisome signs on the horizon. The success of prominent television preachers inspired others to enter the medium. Often they adopted the same program format. Competition for Sunday time slots went up, and so did the costs. By 1985, as more and more programs vied for viewer support, Rex Humbard found his revenues falling behind rising prices for airtime. Stations across the country canceled his program, and the following year he folded his TV tent after thirty-three years on the air. Since the 1970s, he had forsaken the pressure to build ever larger buildings, and in a 1986 interview Humbard sadly said, "People will not give a dollar to win a soul or bring a person to a saving knowledge of Jesus Christ. They give their dollars to build giant cathedrals, projects, schools."

Within a few years, syndicated religious broadcasters had faded from secular TV, driven by rising costs either to radio or to Christian-owned television that could deliver consistently supportive evangelical audiences. The day when syndicated preachers could buy airtime across immense networks of local stations was gone. Cable and satellite technology promised unprecedented geographic outreach and twenty-four-hour daily coverage. Yet as cable systems grew and households gained unprecedented program choices, the viewing public was fragmenting—with the potential that gospel programs might be consigned to a "religious channel ghetto" seen only by Christians.

As "televangelists" prospered and expanded their ministries through viewer support, success brought public scrutiny. People outside the evangelical audience saw only the fund-raising appeals and "flashy" building projects. During the decade, public opinion of gospel broadcasters plummeted. By 1987, a *New York Times* poll found two-thirds of the American public had an unfavorable view of television preachers, while 90 percent in a *USA Today* survey disapproved of their fund-raising techniques and 71 percent said TV evangelists in general were out to enrich themselves.

Yet as 1987 dawned, the evangelical tide seemed to be surging like a flood. Vast media resources were available to bind the Christian community into a cohesive social and political movement. After a decade of tasting power, the final outcome seemed at hand. One of their own, a leader in religious broadcasting, was the front-runner for the presidency of the United States. In February, Pat Robertson emerged from nowhere to defeat the incumbent vice president, George Bush, in the Michigan Republican caucuses. In March, the Robertson campaign seemed right on track.

Then came the news from Oklahoma.

8

THE CRISIS COMES

1987–1994

Oral Roberts saw a vision of Jesus. It was nine hundred feet tall and it talked to him. It told the Tulsa preacher he was destined to complete his City of Faith research complex. He could reassure supporters their donations would not be wasted. That was seven years ago, in 1980. The City of Faith was saved. And later, Roberts heard another message of confirmation from God, that the City of Faith was ordained to find a cure for cancer. But in the years of its construction, as fund-raising appeals took a growing share of airtime, Roberts lost (between 1980 and 1986) nearly two-thirds of his television audience. Fewer viewers meant declining donations. By January 1987, the situation was coming to a crisis. And then God talked to Oral Roberts again.

God would take him home if his followers did not send $8 million by the end of March. When Roberts made the announcement, he was serious. He sent out millions of letters, informing his supporters that March would be his last month on earth unless they responded. As the word went out, the media descended upon his doorstep. They called it "Donate or I Die," "Your Money or My Life," and laughed that God was holding hostages for ransom. But Roberts stood firm. He told television viewers that he had physically and actually wrestled with the devil. He went up to the prayer tower at Oral Roberts University to remain until the money was raised. They didn't understand. Neither did the public. In a *USA Today* survey, 98 percent of those who expressed an opinion said they did not believe God had given Oral Roberts a deadline to raise $8 million. Yet he made it, accepting the final $1.3 million from the owner of a Florida racetrack.

But the public never did understand. And in the outcry, reporters barely noticed another story that came across the wires. Tammy Faye Bakker, cohost of the PTL Network *Jim and Tammy TV Ministry Hour*, was checking into the Betty Ford Center in Palm Springs, California, to undergo treatment for addiction to prescription drugs. The reporters were still camped out in Tulsa, counting down the days for Oral Roberts, when an even bigger story beckoned. It had sex, sleaze, hush money. Things they could understand.

Rise of a Shooting Star

Of all the religious broadcasters in America, Jim Bakker was the industry's shooting star. For four years he lived on the road, an itinerant evangelist, preaching for souls and gas money. Then he met Pat Robertson in 1965, joined the fledgling Christian Broadcasting Network, and rose from kid-show puppeteer to cohost of *The 700 Club*. After a brief role in helping launch the Trinity Broadcasting Network, in 1974 he was hired as president of PTL Television, begun that year with $52 in the bank. Within five years the network, based in Charlotte, North Carolina, was carried by satellite twenty-four hours a day to cable systems across America. Airtime was purchased for *The PTL Club* on some two hundred stations—"more affiliates than the ABC network," as Bakker liked to say—while international editions were aired on five continents.

The offices and studios of PTL (for "Praise the Lord" or "People That Love") were housed in an enlarged replica of the original Burton Parish Church at Williamsburg, Virginia. Outside of town, the ministry maintained a 1400-acre complex with landscaped grounds, a Christian academy, and a "Total Living Center" for any of the two hundred thousand PTL "partners" who might visit Charlotte for a telecast. Ground was broken in 1978 for Heritage USA, later to become the nation's third most-visited theme park (though no admission was charged). Annual broadcast revenues in 1979 topped $51 million, more than Pat Robertson, Jerry Falwell, or any other television ministry in America.

In its way, the meteoric rise of Jim Bakker mirrored the explosive growth of the religious broadcasting industry. His father was a machine repairman at a piston ring factory in Muskegon, Michigan, and a devout man in the Assemblies of God church. But it took the trauma of an auto accident, at age eighteen, to turn young Bakker to Christ. He enrolled in Bible college, but left school in 1961 to marry a pretty coed—he and Tammy Faye LaValley were engaged on their third date—and began four years of itinerant preaching.

However, as the PTL network soared to the forefront of gospel television, by 1979 criticism also began to surface. That year fourteen PTL vice presidents departed the ministry, including the executive vice president who originally founded PTL and hired Bakker to be its president in 1974. Bakker selected a new executive vice president, replaced the board of directors, and was himself confirmed "for life" as president and chairman of the board. While 120 employees were laid off, his parents and brother and sister were maintained on the payroll.

In the early months of 1979, Bakker admitted to his TV audience that the organization had run up at least $10 million of red ink. Though a major telethon staved off certain bankruptcy, many local stations threatened to cancel *The PTL Club* for slow payment and complained of its highly emotional fund-raising appeals. At the same time, the ministry faced an FCC investigation over charges that Bakker had sought donations for one purpose and used them for another—a violation of the law, if true. The evangelist refused to cooperate with investigators, vowing to fight the FCC on constitutional grounds. When former ministry executives stepped forward to corroborate the allegations, Bakker blamed *them* for the management mess. After all, he replied, that's why they were fired.

For three years, the FCC investigated the allegations of fraudulent fund-raising. When its report was completed in December 1982, the agency took two actions. First, the FCC by law could only assess penalties against broadcast stations, and PTL owned only one. (The ministry purchased an Ohio station in 1977 but, after Bakker raised $1 million in pledges from local viewers, abandoned plans to build a new studio and fired most of the staff.) Thus the FCC inquiry was ended that month, after the agency allowed PTL to transfer station ownership to another evangelical broadcaster. The FCC also submitted its findings to the U.S. Justice Department, but in March 1983 the Criminal Division declined to prosecute.

Headlines They Never Intended

The incident, however, brought PTL more scrutiny than ever before. The Bakkers had always projected an intensely emotional, even sensational, screen personality. Now they were getting attention, and making headlines, with a regularity they never intended.

March 1983: Articles in *The Charlotte Observer* confirm that PTL purchased for Bakker and his family a Florida waterfront condominium, even as the ministry laid off some one hundred employees. The paper also reports that PTL paid for a European trip on the Concorde supersonic airliner for Bakker and ten others.

October 1983: A report by the *Orlando Sentinel Star* discloses that Bakker had checked into a luxury Florida hotel, spending four days in a five-bedroom suite costing a thousand dollars a day.

October 1984: *The Charlotte Observer* reports that as the Bakkers pleaded with viewers for $5 million, the couple acquired a Palm Springs vacation home, a Mercedes-Benz, and a Rolls Royce. "We just had to have a little place of our own," Bakker told reporters. He explained to the *Chicago Tribune*, "It would be phony for me to drive an inexpensive car to convince people to give me money." His salary was not paid by PTL viewers but by the church he founded. "I make a nice salary and I know I earn it. What would you pay a man to raise $100 million a year? What's that worth?"

October 1985: A review of PTL accounting procedures is launched by the Evangelical Council for Financial Accountability, a watchdog agency created in 1979 to promote voluntary self-regulation. The investigation follows published reports that the ministry was $6 million in debt despite 1984 revenues of $66 million.

December 1986: PTL reports record annual revenues of $129 million. Yet the media points out that, at the same time, the ministry laid off one-quarter of its workforce.

Despite the crises and controversy, by 1987 the PTL organization encompassed an astonishing array of operations. "The Inspirational Network" carried twenty-four-hour religious programming produced at PTL's modern studios and sent to 1300 cable systems serving nearly fifteen million homes. *The Jim and Tammy TV Ministry Hour* aired on some 170 stations nationwide. The ministry operated from 2300 acres, just south of Charlotte in Fort Mill, South Carolina. The complex featured a broadcast training school, Christian academy, and ministry centers for prison outreach, drug rehabilitation, and crisis pregnancy assistance. A modern resort center did a brisk business in vacation homes, condominiums, time-share units, and retirement housing.

And the jewel in the PTL crown was the Heritage USA theme park. With 6.1 million visitors reported in 1986, only Disney World and Disneyland could boast more attendance. Some 1100 hotel rooms and campsites were available, with 1500 on the drawing board—including 513 rooms at the sumptuous twenty-one-story Heritage Grand Towers. Bakker also envisioned a "Bible Land" park, complete with a replica of Old Jerusalem, and predicted that by 1992 Heritage USA would be a Christian community of 30,000 residents. With the Heritage Grand Towers pushing upward, even the sky seemed no limit to Jim Bakker. When his birthday came that year, January 2, 1987, the forty-seven-year-old evangelist cele-brated by breaking ground for his biggest dream yet: the largest church in the world, a $100 million replica of London's Crystal Palace, able to seat thirty thousand worshipers under a single roof. "The only assurance that we'll be able to build it," he declared to an enthusiastic crowd, "is the fact that everything else . . . [at PTL] has been built and paid for as it was finished." God had called him to the task and now, "I've fallen in love with this building. It's an obsession. I will either build this building or I will die trying." Then standing at the palace's future front entrance, he added, "Just wait and see. The best is yet to come."

Seventy-seven days later, however, the PTL president and chair-man "for life" had resigned.

Who Did the Manipulating?

When Jim Bakker announced his resignation to reporters on March 19, 1987, the national press had a field day. The story had everything! A flashy celebrity evangelist, a twenty-one-year-old church secretary, and a Florida motel room—with charges of black-mail and hints of dark power plots thrown in for good measure.

That day Bakker was the picture of a simple minister brought low by unscrupulous enemies jealous of his good works. "Tammy Faye and I, and our ministries, have been subjected to constant harassment and pressures by various groups and forces whose objective has been to undermine and destroy us," he told reporters. Now his foes had driven the couple to where "[our] physical and emotional resources have been so overwhelmed that we are presently under full-time therapy."

As for the woman who claimed to have sex with him seven years ago, on December 6, 1980, Bakker neither confirmed nor denied the incident but told reporters, "I categorically deny that I've ever sexually assaulted or harassed anyone." It was true, however, that he had been "wickedly manipulated by treacherous former friends" who conspired for blackmail "to betray me into a sexual encounter" and who "victimized me with the aid of a female confederate."

Yes, he had paid the woman $115,000 in 1985 "to avoid further suffering or hurt to anyone, to appease these persons who were determined to destroy the ministry." Yet in hindsight, he realized, "We ought to have exposed the blackmailers to the penalties of the law." Even now he was not resigning because of the charges against him but was stepping down—while he could still name a successor—to thwart a "diabolical" takeover plot by a prominent (and unnamed) rival evangelist.

The truth, however, was somewhat different from the picture Bakker presented. Later he changed the story of his sexual sin, saying it was arranged voluntarily to make his wife jealous during a time of marital trouble. Thus could Bakker claim he never "assaulted" anyone. The "diabolical plot" was a July 1986 request by Jimmy Swaggart, a fellow Assemblies of God minister, that the denomination check rumors of misconduct against Bakker that could lead to a scandal that might tarnish the church by association.

Swaggart learned the *Charlotte Observer* planned to expose Bakker. The fiery Louisiana preacher, whose *Jimmy Swaggart* program from Baton Rouge was the highest-rated religious telecast in America, then began the biblical process described in Matthew 18. First he obtained a personal meeting in February 1987 with top Bakker aide Richard Dortch. When the session brought only denial, Swaggart prepared the next biblical step by asking two witnesses, broadcasters Jerry Falwell and John Ankerberg, to join him for a second meeting. But it was too late. The scandal by then had become public.

The Worst-Case Scenario

In resigning his position, Bakker turned over the PTL ministries to Jerry Falwell. One was a charismatic preacher, the other an independent Baptist. But the two were long acquainted in broadcasting circles. Most important, Falwell understood the potential harm to *all* broadcasters from any scandal and felt burdened of God to help restore confidence by keeping PTL viable and functioning. Thus, in naming a new board of directors, he reached out to respected leaders from both the fundamentalist and charismatic traditions.

The *Old Time Gospel Hour* evangelist had great respect for what Bakker had built at PTL. But Falwell and his team could not close their eyes to the mounting evidences they uncovered of financial abuse, as deeply troubling as any sexual indiscretions. Exorbitant salaries and bonuses paid to the Bakkers, their relatives, and friends. Few coherent accounting records. Estimated debts of $70 million to 1400 creditors, $23 million of it delinquent. The Heritage Grand Towers unfinished, its contractors owed $14 million, though more than enough was raised for its completion.

And the "Lifetime Partners." Each sent $1,000 to build the Towers, on the promise of receiving three nights lodging per year for the rest of their lives. Among Christian ministries, many projects are funded this way. But Bakker had sold 120,000 partnerships to build a hotel with only 513 rooms. In the face of such fraud, Falwell politely but firmly informed Bakker his ministry with PTL was over.

In the months that followed, the American public saw a soap opera more bizarre and sensational than anything in a Hollywood script. Bakker charged Falwell with betrayal and plotting to take over PTL. Investigations were launched by the IRS, the FBI, the

Justice Department, the Postal Service, the South Carolina Tax Commission, and the United States Congress. Yet Falwell fought hard to keep PTL afloat. The summer of 1987 saw the best attendance ever at Heritage USA, while a reorganization plan went steadily forward under the bankruptcy laws.

But the Bakkers weren't through, not yet. Friends of the deposed PTL president went to court, seeking the right to file a competing reorganization plan of their own. When their petition was granted, the direction of the troubled ministry was thrown into doubt. Efforts of the new leadership to restore stability and public confidence were for naught. Falwell and the board promptly resigned, ending the best chance for the PTL organization to survive.

In the end, Bakker became the tragicomic star of a humiliating public trial, given forty-five years (later reduced to eight) for his financial misconduct. Tammy Faye tried to carry on in a storefront church, but she at last divorced her husband of nearly thirty years. Jimmy Swaggart fell into a scandal of his own, admitting in February 1988 that he had immoral liaisons with a prostitute. And Jerry Falwell, a month after resigning from PTL, announced he would step down as head of the Moral Majority and return full-time to pastoral ministry, "rededicating my life to preaching the gospel."

Echoes of the PTL scandal reverberated far and wide. Christian ministries across America saw steep declines in giving. Within ninety days after the Bakker scandal erupted, Falwell and Swaggart each reported donations to their ministries were down more than $2 million per month. Pat Robertson told CBN viewers that quarterly revenues were off $12 million. His own nascent presidential campaign was caught in the backlash, as voters who "leaned against" Robertson rose as high as 70 percent in national polls. Public disapproval of televangelists rose to more than 90 percent in numerous surveys. Religious broadcasting now faced the second great crisis of its history.

Second Crisis, Same Issue

Attorney Richard Wiley had always been a friend of religious broadcasting. Not only because of his Christian faith, but because he firmly believed that religious broadcasts were truly in the public interest. The Federal Communications Commission classified them that way, and during his term as chairman, he had steadfastly upheld the policy within the dictates of the law. When he returned to private practice and NRB asked him to advise the association as its general counsel, to him the assignment was an extension of his lifelong commitment to public service. With his knowledge of communications law, and his status and contacts as former head of the FCC, he had helped Christian broadcasters on many vital issues. But now was the real test, an issue that went to the very fight for which NRB was founded.

As he squeezed through the crowded room and into his seat that morning in October 1987, Wiley knew the stakes. Could religious broadcasters be trusted with free access to the airwaves? After the explosive revelations of the PTL scandal, many were calling for new regulations and oversight. For months the nation had been transfixed by the soap opera from Charlotte, and now the drama moved to Washington. Reporters lined up for hours to get into the hearing room of the House Ways and Means Committee. Wiley winced at the harsh glare of the TV lights, tried to shut his ears to the roaring buzz around him. When Congressman J. J. Pickle, the Texas Democrat who chaired the Oversight Subcommittee, gaveled the session to order, Wiley was relieved to get started.

"While the IRS has powerful tools for enforcing financial honesty, we believe that, in this area that is fraught with sensitive First Amendment concerns, it is far preferable for religious broadcasters to put their own house in order. . . . For this reason, we would like to suggest that the need for, or the composition of, any congressional hearings be reassessed when this private initiative has unfolded." Wiley had spoken those words last July when he had accompanied NRB executive director Ben Armstrong, NRB president Robert Cook of *The King's Hour* broadcast, and twenty-five other broadcasters in a private meeting with Congressman Pickle to discuss his recently announced plans for a hearing. Though Armstrong had worried at first that the inquiry might be "a new inquisition," NRB decided to sit down and work with the chairman—a strategy the association had employed successfully since its earliest days.

Congress Keeps a Promise?

They reassured Pickle that PTL was the exception, not the rule; that they were vitally anxious to put down shady operators who gave the industry a black eye; that they had upheld a code of ethics since 1944; and that as huge ministry conglomerates emerged over the past decade, NRB had begun—before the PTL scandal—to strengthen its code enforcement. In 1978 the association promulgated a tough "Principles and Guidelines for Fund-raising, Accounting, and Financial Reporting." In 1979 it encouraged broadcasters to voluntarily submit to the newly formed Evangelical Council for Financial Accountability. And in 1986 the NRB board approved formation of a new Ethics and Financial Integrity Commission (EFICOM) with enhanced authority for getting broadcasters to regulate themselves.

Congressman Pickle listened at that July meeting with genuine interest. For his part, the Texas lawmaker reassured the NRB delegation he was not looking for a witch-hunt. His panel would only explore how tax-exempt status is applied to various aspects of Christian broadcast operations.

To do that, Pickle explained, subcommittee members wanted help in learning how diverse ministries account for and then allocate donations to specific areas. Wiley assured the congressman that "subject to constitutional concerns regarding the separation of church and state, we are committed to cooperating fully with the legitimate inquiries of your [House Ways and Means Oversight] Subcommittee."

It had been a good meeting. And now, in October, Wiley felt cautiously confident as the actual hearings began. The NRB leadership had made good on its pledge to Congressman Pickle, working through the summer to put the EFICOM structure into place before the subcommittee hearings got started. And the association had been active on other fronts to restore confidence and stave off new government regulations. NRB mounted an aggressive education campaign as public interest gave its members the chance to place articles in major periodicals such as USA Today and the Wall Street Journal. The effort to correct stereotypes of televangelists was aided by new surveys that showed top TV preachers averaged less than 11 percent of their broadcast time for fund-raising—half the time given to commercials on secular television. And an NRB Defense Fund had been created so a quick response could be mounted as the challenge continued to unfold.

Broadcasters had done their part. But chairman Pickle was under intense pressure to "do something" in response to the PTL scandal. The hearings offered him a national platform. And with the public's current disdain for television preachers, gospel broadcasters were an easy target for any politician. Would the subcommittee be able to resist the outcry and the temptation to widen the investigation? Perhaps even to examine religious organizations and churches in general, to explore sensitive matters of ministry content and practice, and whether their activities should be subject to government sanction?

A Change in Administration

When the hearings were over, broadcasters were mostly satisfied, thankful that J. J. Pickle had kept his promise to confine the inquiry to tax issues and avoid "a new inquisition." The months ahead set the pattern as Congress and the Administration declined sweeping changes, directing the IRS instead to work out cases privately with individual ministries under existing law. The policy was dramatically reaffirmed at the 1988 NRB convention in Washington, as President Ronald Reagan and Vice President George Bush both appeared to celebrate the special relationship they had built with religious broadcasters since 1980. When George Bush succeeded to the White House a year later, he, too, gave broadcasters the chance to police themselves.

But could they do it? The industry showed its resolve as the 1988 NRB convention voted its approval for the establishment of EFICOM. And they gave the panel a powerful new tool. In addition to following general ethical principles, broadcasters seeking the "seal of approval" must meet specific criteria—for finances, accounting, fund-raising, and governance—that could be objectively measured. And the program would be administered by the Evangelical Council for Financial Accountability, an independent agency with a decade of experience as a Christian ministry watchdog.

Then in 1989, even as Washington witnessed a change in administration, so did change come to National Religious Broadcasters. With EFICOM firmly established as a credible agency, Ben Armstrong stepped down after twenty-three years of service to NRB, knowing he had helped to successfully bring the industry to its greatest growth and (after the battle over paid versus sustaining time) he had led through the second great crisis of its history in securing—at least for now—the precious freedom of the airwaves. Now as with Moses, it was time for others to cross over, to battle for the restoration of public confidence.

Symbol of a New Direction

Brandt Gustavson surveyed the floor of the Los Angeles Convention Center. Nearly five thousand broadcasters and exhibitors filled the hall, their voices rising and falling in a continuing buzz. The 1993 NRB convention was the first held outside Washington in twenty-six years. That was significant. Three years ago, when he was named executive director, the idea of convening anywhere but Washington was unthinkable. In the shadow of scandal and crisis, religious broadcasters had to keep their fences mended where it counted.

But now Los Angeles! Gustavson had been involved with NRB through virtually his entire career, for more than thirty years, first as an executive in the Moody Radio Network and later at Trans World Radio. He had held many NRB offices, moved through the chairs, served three years as president. And all through those years, through all those Washington conventions, religious broadcasters had seen their struggle on a *political* level, of making the right friends and pushing the right policies. Now the trek to Los Angeles, to the heart of Hollywood, suggested a new direction. Now broadcasters of the gospel were ready to go beyond, to the next level, to make their case for access to the airwaves on a *cultural* level. Not just convincing people in the right places, but convincing the American public.

And the battle was going forward. In six years since the PTL scandal, Gustavson had seen gospel radio and television continue to grow. New crises could happen, but the potential for abuse was, he thought, being addressed in some ways by the marketplace. The success of TV preachers had increased competition for time slots and viewers. Now it wasn't so easy to build vast networks of television stations around any single *program* or personality. Radio was booming as a lower-cost alternative. And Christian *networks* that delivered consistent and responsive audiences were becoming the driving force of gospel television. The major religious networks were now professionally staffed corporations and not personal empires. CBN had kept right on going, for example, when Pat Robertson left for a time to run for president.

Then too, the public outcry for accountability was too loud to ignore. Prodded by EFICOM, most broadcasters saw sensitivity to public concern as key to their survival. All types of Christian organizations took the lesson to heart. By 1993 the Evangelical Council for Financial Accountability represented members with more than $1 billion of income. Gustavson knew EFICOM was the right response for the right time. And God had turned the PTL scandal to good, using it to build ECFA into a position of authority. Now the agency was capable of taking over the role of EFICOM, allowing NRB to focus its resources on serving rather than policing its members. For that reason, delegates to the NRB Los Angeles convention voted to replace EFICOM with a requirement that all major broadcasters join ECFA—and meet its criteria—to remain members in good standing of NRB.

When it came to another area—the role of broadcasters in the political arena—Gustavson liked what he saw. For two decades, national politics had brought gospel preachers both influence *and* scrutiny. The PTL explosion, by itself a sensation, was certainly heightened by media anxiety over the "hidden agenda" of TV evangelists. Yet the election of George Bush meant the Republican nomination wouldn't be up for grabs until 1996. Instead the evangelical movement was arming for the future, building its base at the local level. And broadcasters, who had planted the seeds during the 1970s and 1980s, could now leave the work to a growing army of Christian activist organizations.

Some Things Never Change

Brandt Gustavson took his seat. He had learned about the congressional hearing only yesterday and rushed back from a meeting in Dallas to testify. At least the flight gave him a few hours to go over the remarks that had been hurriedly drafted and typed for the session. Now he could only wait patiently for the rap of the gavel. Besides, it was good to get his breath. The hearing room of the House Energy and Commerce Committee wasn't too crowded. It was only a subcommittee meeting. But for religious broadcasters, it was important to be there. In his years of NRB service, Gustavson had been to the White House under four presidents, had made the rounds of Capitol Hill more times than he could remember. And as he waited for the hearing to begin, he had an ironic thought.

It had been fifty years. Each trial had come and gone, the sternest test last. But after half a century, gospel preachers were part of the fabric of American radio and television. Even in the awful after-math of the PTL scandal, the public, the press, and the policy mak-ers had questioned only the *responsibility* and not the *right* of evan-gelists who use the airwaves. No one demanded, as they had fifty years ago, that preachers be banned from purchasing airtime. How-ever, he was also afraid. Fifty years was a long time. Most Chris-tians today had grown up with religious radio and television. They took it for granted. It had always been around, and they assumed it always would be. They had never known a time when freedom to broadcast the gospel had ever been questioned, had ever been fought for. After all, this was America. Hadn't Christian broad-casters always been free? Wasn't it in the Constitution?

Yet even as National Religious Broadcasters prepared to mark its fiftieth anniversary, here he was. This time it was a bill to rein-state the abolished Fairness Doctrine, a law that could force Chris-tian stations to offer free airtime to abortionists, homosexuals, and other proponents of liberal viewpoints. Earlier, it had been an FCC action about cable operators who refused to allocate channels to local Christian stations in their viewing areas.

But his thoughts were interrupted. The gavel sounded. It was time. "Mr. Chairman," he began, "in making this argument for reli-gious liberty . . ."

Epilogue
THE WORD ENDURES

2044

John Q. Christian pulled into the driveway. After sitting on the Central Expressway for thirty minutes, he was fuming. He paid good money for the NaviSat console, just to avoid jams like this! It would have told him about the accident on the interchange. Then he could have taken the Reagan Bridge and gone the back way home. But the blank map grid stared at him from the dashboard, useless because the garage couldn't get the right part until next week. Really! Like his dad always used to say, "If they can put a man on Mars, then you'd think they could . . ."

Well, there had been nothing to do but wait out the traffic. At least the CMX was working right. Signing up for the service, now *that* was a good investment! Worth every decimal on the debit card. Just punch in a quick fax home so Donna could keep his dinner warm, then dial up the Cellular Music Express to help him relax. The Christian waveband had a library of music and teaching like you wouldn't believe! Everything from Christian fusion (he couldn't stand that stuff) to the complete audio books of Oswald Chambers.

He even had a friend at church who was taking a CMX car-study course in biblical counseling. But John wasn't such a serious type. He'd become a big fan of the recent Southern Gospel music revival, and it was fun to dial up an old concert, digitally rebuilt from the original LPs (what were those?), and hear the great old quartets— right in his car—more clearly than if he'd been there a hundred years ago. And CMX was a lot better than the way mom and dad used to rummage around the glove compartment, picking out beat-up cassettes of their favorite songs. Of course, even with his CMX, John still listened to the radio. For spontaneity and current events, you couldn't beat the many Christian talk shows, news features, and teaching programs on the radio dial.

Donna kissed him warmly at the door. Being a homemaker was definitely a skilled occupation these days, and John often marveled at how much Donna got done. Though the InterAct unit down in the den was a great electronic time-saver, she had her hands full each day arranging everything from grocery deliveries to debit transactions. Through the FiberLight network, InterAct could locate anything from insurance policies to school clothes anywhere in the world. But it took Donna herself, through research and just plain hard work, to find the best bargains for their family.

Once, they decided to find out how much Donna saved them. They switched the InterAct from video to computer mode so it could track her purchases and financial transactions for the year to date. When the unit showed the comparison to market prices, they couldn't believe it! Since then Donna had programmed the

InterAct to run a weekly report so she could track her performance. Now she was saving even more. Home was truly a window to the world, and a mother could do just about anything. Some church families even used the InterAct to homeschool their children. And John sometimes used it for telecommuting, though he generally preferred the discipline of working in an office.

Since he was home late, the kids had decided not to wait for him. He could hear Mark and Laura squealing in the rec room, trying out a new Pretendo game on the InterAct. (It was a good thing they had three units in the house.) Well, at least Donna knew about it. Just last week John read on the daily FaxNews printout about some kids who found the family access code and ran up a huge Pretendo debit without their parents knowing. Hmm, what if it had been the LoveClub instead? Now *that* was a scary thought! For that matter, though, John sometimes wondered where all the information went about their own family purchases, transactions, and entertainment choices. He hoped the Communications Privacy Act was enough protection. But where did all those E-junk companies get his name?

But John had been looking forward to this evening all week. As a family they tried not to watch too much on the InterAct. After all, it was technically possible for the system to deliver five hundred channels, though there was not enough of an audience to support that many. The major Christian networks had a lot of good programs. And every night after supper they watched *Videvotions* together. But John and Donna preferred to spend most evenings either at church or in family activities. Yet once a week Donna arranged a special entertainment program.

Usually she punched in an order for an educational program or a favorite movie, after checking it out on the preview channel. Mark and Laura loved the way they could make choices (when they could agree!) at different points in the story, as if they were characters themselves. Often Grandma would join in, watching and playing along on the InterAct in her own house. She loved it more than the kids! She still remembered when Dad had to leave home and rent a "video" from a store. (Though for some reason she said the worst part was figuring out how to use some machine called a VCR. John had seen some once in a museum.)

Mom also said that anyone watching a channel could only see what the channel was broadcasting. Of course, many channels still operated that way today. But on others you could access the channel's library and punch in the programs *you* wanted to see. Kind of like renting one of those old videos without leaving home. The Choice Channel had some great Christian programs, and John loved their slogan, "Many are called, and many are chosen."

But tonight they had a special treat. While the children had Pretendo to keep them busy, Donna had rented a couple of V-suits for the evening. The fee was a bit high—though the store delivered—yet the experience was worth it! John and Donna had been studying Bible prophecy in their adult *Videvotions* group. Now with these virtual reality suits, they could stroll down the computer-simulated streets of Old Jerusalem, feel the stones of the Eastern Gate, or hear the wind across the vast plain of Armageddon, as if they were actually there. What a tremendous help that would be for their Bible study!

Later that evening, as he donned his V-suit, several thoughts came into John's mind. With the InterAct and the CMX and all the things he took for granted, was he getting too absorbed in his own activities? Was the family spending enough time in the community, getting to know others, developing relationships that witnessed Christ? Somehow he recalled doing more of that when he was a boy. Even trips to the video store were a chance to meet neighbors. But now you just punched in commands to the InterAct.

And church? Though John and Donna attended faithfully, they didn't see many friends outside of Sundays and Wednesdays. John had to admit that. Were they letting the InterAct supply the "fellowship" they needed? Did it leave less time for having friends over? For prayer? For Bible reading? Or was it a way to connect with teaching resources from all over the world—aids that enhanced their Christian life that they could obtain no other way?

John wondered. Then he recalled how last week *Videvotions* had gone over different prophecies in the Bible about signs that would take place as the end of time drew near. From Daniel 12:4 he had read, "Knowledge shall be increased." That would be one of the signs. As John wriggled into his V-suit, pulled on the gloves, and adjusted the compuvisor over his eyes, he wondered if that time might be soon.

Four Vital Issues

Information highways. Fiber-optic networks. High-definition television. Interactive television. Virtual reality. Advances in everything from computers and compact discs to cable television and cellular communications. All these technologies, and many more, are just over the horizon. And each has vast potential for evil, for good, and for propagation of the gospel in ways yet unimagined. Like radio in the 1920s, television in the 1940s, and cable in the 1960s, decisions are being made in the 1990s that will shape the new broadcast media for generations to come. Today, government and industry are wrestling over four vital issues.

Issue 1: Who will wire it? The idea of network radio, of programs broadcast jointly by stations across the country, was demonstrated as early as 1922. Yet regular network broadcasting did not happen until 1927, when NBC and CBS went on the air. Only then, when AT&T decided to sell off its own radio stations, did the giant telephone conglomerate open its long-distance lines to broadcasters. More recently, the development of cable television might have been very different, if not for the court-ordered breakup of the Bell System opening a niche for independent cable operators.

Today, fiber-optic cables are being installed across the country. Able to carry almost unlimited information on a beam of light, fiber optics provide the network capacity needed for the coming communications revolution. Someday, planners say, the nation will be linked by vast "information highways" built of fiber-optic cable. But who will install these networks? Telephone companies? Cable operators? Giant media conglomerates? The government?

For that matter, the future could just as easily be wireless. National cellular communications networks are developing. The 1993 launching of the first direct broadcast satellite (DBS) services allows 150 channels to be beamed to portable home dishes only eighteen inches wide. And through "digital compression," over-the-air stations can broadcast eight channels over the same signal that now handles only one.

Already the scramble is on. Local phone companies have the advantage of nearly 100 percent penetration into American households, yet they must still spend billions to replace their existing lines with fiber-optic cables. Cable television penetrates only 60 percent of the nation. But operators are increasing their fiber-optic capacity more swiftly, and in new markets they have the easier task of building new lines rather than replacing old lines.

Observers had predicted war. But by the end of 1993, an incredible "merger mania" took hold that saw no less than five announced partnerships between major cable and telephone companies. The action was paced by the nation's top two cable companies, Tele-Communications, Inc. (TCI), and Time Warner, who proposed to join forces with Bell Atlantic and U. S. West, respectively. (The Bell/TCI merger was later called off.) Yet whatever emerges on the road to building America's information highways, history suggests FCC standards will be needed for those networks to connect into homes through the same optical cables.

Issue 2: What will receive it? Since the first crackle and hiss of a crystal radio set, broadcasting has been profoundly shaped by requirements for public reception. Radio broadcasting grew as homemade sets gave way first to manufactured models, then to dual AM/FM receivers. Television took off in 1947 when the FCC adopted standards for all sets. Five years later the agency authorized a new UHF band, but its potential was not realized until 1964 when Congress required new sets be fitted for both VHF and UHF reception. About the same time, color television became afford-able, with profound effects for broadcasting. And in the 1990s, Congress is talking again about television sets. Current proposals to mandate "V-chips" that let parents block out programs rated for violence may impact broadcasting in ways both profound and unforeseen.

In the 1960s, "picture phones" were the wave of the future, until the Bell System found people preferred their privacy. What broad-cast media might have grown from this technology? Only today is the concept of personal visual communications being revived. In the 1970s, the popularity of Polaroid instant photography spurred Kodak to take the next step. But its "Selectavision" instant movies, which needed a special viewer, were swamped as the public flocked to new videocassette recorders that plugged right into their TV sets. Originally a system for home movies, VCRs ushered in a new entertainment revolution, including new ways to proclaim the gospel of Christ.

Over the past decade, video game systems were linked with tele-vision receivers, opening people's eyes to the potential of "inter-active" media. Yet at the same time, early attempts to hook TV sets into personal computer systems failed, as television receivers were inadequate to the swiftly growing possibilities of consumer software. Nevertheless, the merging of video and computer tech-nology is the heart of the communications revolution.

They call it "interactive media." Sales of interactive CD-ROM compact discs were introduced in 1992. By then America had its first interactive TV network, a California system with a $199 con-trol box and $15 monthly fee that lets users play along with game shows like *Jeopardy!*, predict the winner of the Kentucky Derby, or (for an additional fee) compete for actual prizes. The possibili-ties for someday accessing movies or stock quotes or home shop-ping on demand are endless. But it all depends upon a receiver that displays video like a television, is easy to control like a cable box, yet offers the options of a personal computer.

The rub is the screen. Television sets employ an "interlaced" system that scans pictures by every other line. First it scrolls through even-numbered lines, then repeats for odd ones. That way, only half the picture is scanned at any one time. The technique produces flickering images but, by reducing the electronic demands, helps to make receivers compact and affordable. By contrast, computer monitors employ "progressive" scanning that produces flicker-free images since every line is always scanned.

Computer firms chafe at the limitations of interlaced screens. Yet broadcasters and television manufacturers worry that, if progressive scanning is mandated, costs will rise and development of "high definition television" (HDTV) will be slowed. In 1987, with Japan already far ahead, the FCC established a competition to select an advanced American television standard. A breakthrough came in 1990 when one of the contestants, General Instrument Corporation, bypassed the Japanese "analog" system with a new "digital" method that encodes video signals the same way computer information is processed.

The advance promised not only theater-quality television pictures, but a final merging of video and computer technology. In 1993 the remaining FCC contestants pooled their entries into a single industry proposal. New "smart" televisions would know via digital code whether a picture was interlaced or progressively scanned, and be able to accommodate either format. Current programs could continue, even as upgraded broadcast pictures and computer applications were developed. If the FCC approves and tests are satisfactory, purchasers of the first HDTV sets could cheer the 1996 Summer Olympics in spectacular color.

Issue 3: How will we interact with it? Radio is tuned by a dial, television by a knob or remote, and cable by a box. When the information superhighways of tomorrow are built, how will we interact with the system? How will a homemaker order school clothes or a checking account balance? A dad arrange a movie or get the latest sports scores? A child receive video math tutoring or look up a database encyclopedia reference? Will they dial a phone, press a remote, or sit down to a computer keyboard?

Far from idle speculation, every element for a new interactive medium is potentially in place today. For example, in 1992 TCI announced that its cable system, the largest in the nation, would adopt the digital technology of General Instrument Corporation. Then General Instrument joined with computer giants Intel and Microsoft to develop a new remote control unit that is actually a handheld personal computer, able to manage interactive data from more than five hundred channels. When the unit is ready, an alliance between TCI and a major telephone company could bring the technology into one out of every three or four American homes.

Issue 4: Who will monitor it? The troubling issue of the communication revolution is privacy. When consumers access and use the new interactive media, those interactions must be transmitted and electronically stored for service providers to act upon. Someone could build formidable files on individuals and families by finding out their choices for entertainment, purchases, finances, perhaps even video voting and opinion polls.

Such information could be used for purposes as benign as census taking, as annoying as marketing, and as ignoble as spying or blackmail. The same privacy issues are at stake, of course, in banking and credit services or in the buying and selling of mailing lists. But against the unimaginable flood of data coursing through the veins of a global interactive network, can any privacy protections be effective? Or would an effective policing system be a cure worse than the disease?

Creation and Evolution

And what does all this mean for religious broadcasting? Will gospel broadcasters find a place as the electric church goes interactive? Should the Lord tarry, the prospects for reaching the world through interactive Bible studies, on-demand Christian music and video, and many more innovations are limitless. Here the past can be a guide. From the historic development of radio, television, cable, and satellite broadcasting, patterns emerge that suggest how the new media of tomorrow may grow and evolve.

Phase 1: The medium emerges. Laboratory research. Experimental transmissions. The work reaches a critical mass, ready to burst upon the public scene, sparked by a major event that captivates consumer imagination and dramatically spotlights the potential of the new medium. The flame ignites. The rush is on!

Experimental radio stations were on the air by 1915. The technology steadily advanced, until regular transmissions were at last possible. Yet not until 1920, when KDKA Pittsburgh electrified the nation with its dramatic coverage of the Harding-Cox presidential election, did the American public awake to the possibilities of radio. The medium mushroomed. More radio stations fueled a market for more radio sets. Then more sets boosted prospects for more stations. It was a self-reinforcing cycle.

The first public television transmission occurred in the 1920s. But it was only an interesting experiment, not ready to go public. A decade later, however, the national love affair with science was on display at the 1939 New York World's Fair. When President Franklin Roosevelt opened the event by television, public excitement knew no bounds. Applications for new television stations poured into the FCC. World War II put a temporary halt to further development, but when it ended, the new medium grew swiftly. Satellite technology burst upon the American public with the Soviet Sputnik launch of 1957. A few years later, its communications potential was unforgettably etched in the minds of millions who watched by television as Apollo astronauts reached toward the moon.

In each medium, religious broadcasters were among the first to see the potential for proclaiming the gospel of Christ. At first, a few pioneer preachers showed the way. Gospel radio had its Paul Rader and R. R. Brown. Television its Rex Humbard, Oral Roberts, and Jerry Falwell. Satellite its Pat Robertson, Paul Crouch, and

Jim Bakker. Then in swift succession scores of evangelical ministries plunged into the new medium to claim it for Christ.

Perhaps some transcending event—maybe a pioneering HDTV broadcast of the 1996 Olympics, or a fad craze over a new video game channel (set to debut in 1994)—will awaken the public to the new possibilities. And when the day of interactive media dawns, its potential for evangelism will be demonstrated by a few innovative and entrepreneurial ministry leaders, ready to take a risk and step out in faith. Then, in abundance, others will swiftly follow.

Phase 2: The medium purges. In wild proliferation, perhaps without regulation, broadcasters rush to stake their claim and establish their territory. Developments move rapidly and new directions are difficult to anticipate. With a lack of adequate standards and coherent guidelines, chaos threatens. In the early years of radio, as stations freely changed signals and hours to suit their needs, the airwaves became a bedlam. Listeners found it nearly impossible to get a clear signal or find their favorite programs. Creation of the Federal Radio Commission in 1927 brought order, but also forced out many station operators—including many religious groups—who could not meet agency standards for professional operation.

Chaos reigned also in the early age of television. Due to wartime restrictions, only six commercial stations were on the air through 1945. But that year, when the FCC lifted the freeze, license applications poured in for 150 new stations. Soon, however, many had second thoughts. Mass production of television receivers, halted during the war, had already been delayed because the FCC set no standards until 1941 (when the agency endorsed interlaced scanning in a picture frame of 525 lines). With few sets in the hands of the public, the market was small—and the costs high—compared to radio, which was then booming.

Color telecasting, begun in 1940–41 by CBS and NBC, threatened to make black-and-white sets obsolete. And the technology for linking local stations to a network through coaxial cables and microwave relays would not be developed until 1949–51. Given these uncertainties, dozens of broadcasters withdrew their license applications. The issue was only resolved when the FCC halted color television in 1947. (Development was stayed until 1953, when the agency declared colorcasting could resume if sets were made to receive both color or monochrome programs. Today the same answer has been proposed so the HDTV can go forward while sets receive both the old and new formats.)

Pay television was introduced in 1951 by the Zenith Radio Corporation, which offered viewers first-run movies by adding a dollar each to their phone bills. Cable television also started in 1949–50 as a means of bringing programs to rural areas. As the pay and cable concepts grew beyond their original scope, however, questions arose. What about signal interference and competition with conventional broadcasters? Could pay and cable really be defined as *broad*casting, and thus subject to FCC rules?

From the past, the pattern is clear. Once a new medium goes public, an initial surge of interest leads to new and unanticipated issues. Whether intended or not, the pattern of government and industry is to plunge ahead, then set standards "as you go" according to public reaction. As a result, the new medium experiences a "shake out" in which only strong, professional operators survive. Interactive media will run into new issues that require new standards, and many early evangelical users of the technology won't be able to keep up.

Phase 3: The medium rationalizes. From the clamor and chaos of a new medium, standards emerge to ensure stability and survival. But that's not all. Stability and survival also require that broadcasters find a rational economic basis for their business. Radio and television were conceived for educational and noncommercial uses. That principle persists in the concept of public ownership of the airwaves, that the spectrum is a limited commodity, a franchise granted to broadcasters who pledge to serve the public interest. Yet it takes money to run a station. Secular radio and television quickly evolved into commercial advertising vehicles, while

Christian radio and television found a rational economic basis in the sale of airtime.

Cable television was first sold to viewers as a way to cut out commercials. Subscribers would underwrite the service rather than advertisers, ensuring responsive community programming. Today it has turned out far differently. Viewers pay chiefly to have a wider selection of channels than is available over the air. Cable operators deliver this selection by paying commercial broadcasters for the right to retransmit their programs. The original concept of community programming has given way to national broadcast organizations, from HBO to ESPN to CNN, that have sprung up to supply programs for cable.

How will the new world of interactive media find an economic basis for survival? As an advertising vehicle? As a service? As a seller of channels? A buyer of programs? Three observations stand out.

First, a broadcast universe of five hundred (or perhaps even one thousand) channels turns the traditional concept of "spectrum scarcity" on its head. The airwaves have always been rationed, by government and by the marketplace, on the idea that space on the radio or television dial is limited. If that basic notion is debunked, how will the economics of the new media be impacted?

Second, a universe of five hundred channels would be likely to fragment the viewing audience into niche markets. The broadcast industry would become like the magazine industry, with specialized offerings that cater to individual subscriber interests. Not long ago, everyone in America watched just three networks. Tomorrow they may watch the Home Improvement Channel, the Chinese Cooking Channel, and the Cat Owners Channel.

At least one outcome, however, seems certain. Interactivity will put more choices into the hands of media consumers. And when they exercise those choices, they will be expected to pay for them. Gospel broadcasters are accustomed to appealing over the air for funds, but tomorrow may see more emphasis on providing fee-based interactive media services. Even today, Christian donors expect to receive books, tapes, or gifts in return for their donations.

Phase 4: The medium nationalizes. The hectic early days are over. The kinks have been worked out, the issues and problems identified, and appropriate standards set to ensure stability and survival. Only now can anyone afford to make the huge investments required to establish national media networks. The NBC and CBS radio networks emerged after the Radio Act of 1927 brought order to the industry. Network television followed in the 1950s, when the basic issues had been resolved and the investment in coaxial cables could move ahead. And cable television has grown more nationalized as the industry matures.

In each of these stages, gospel broadcasters rode the network phenomenon to national prominence. Donald Grey Barnhouse was the first to purchase network radio time. Soon men such as Walter Maier and Charles Fuller achieved national network followings. Percy Crawford was the pioneer in purchasing time on network television. Within a generation, syndicators such as Rex Humbard and Jerry Falwell had learned how to build independent networks of their own. And in the 1980s, as America was wired for cable, broadcasters like Pat Robertson and Jim Bakker won viewers across the country.

Sometime after the turn of the century, the growth of interactive media will give birth to national networks. And when that happens, opportunities for Christian broadcasting on a new scale may abound. Imagine if Donald Barnhouse and *The Bible Study Hour* had been interactive. If *This Is the Life* offered a choice of story endings to fit individual needs. If viewers of the *Hour of Decision* had registered decisions for Christ on their television screens? If the *Rex Humbard World Outreach Ministry* show you missed last week could have been rerun on demand? If those who called *The 700 Club* prayer line could both speak to *and* see their counselor? No doubt, tomorrow will create its own Christian media stars.

Phase 5: The medium grows. Inspired by the success of prominent media preachers, others now rush into the ministry of gospel broadcasting. The astounding early success of Walter Maier and Charles Fuller prompted many more to preach by radio, even as the prominence of Rex Humbard and Oral Roberts inspired other gospel television ministries. Then, as religious broadcasters gain a prominent place in the medium, several things begin to happen. Secular stations and networks fret about controversy and whether preachers are a good risk to pay their bills. The medium now has a solid revenue base, so why bother with religion? Thus new stations and networks spring up, directly owned by Christians to provide outlets for religious broadcasters. And as the electric church grows, as it assumes a higher profile, public scrutiny (and cynicism) of evangelists' motives and lifestyles intensifies.

In the 1940s, radio preachers had catapulted to national attention. Prominence brought scrutiny so that worried network executives put barriers in the way. The controversy over Father Charles Coughlin, a politicized radio priest, seemed to justify their concerns. Yet religious radio continued to grow, aided by new Christian radio networks such as Moody, Northwestern, and Family Radio, and commercially run local Christian stations such as California's KRDU.

Thirty years later the scenario played again, this time with television as the medium. By the 1970s, TV preachers had come to be known as televangelists. They had gained the pinnacle of national prominence. Presidents came to their conventions, politicians sought their favor, new cameras recorded their travels. They raised vast sums, built vast ministries, mobilized vast legions of followers. And the public debated their power. As a legacy from radio, preachers still bought time from local stations rather than from the networks. So Christians went into direct ownership of the medium. The Christian Broadcasting Network, Trinity Broadcasting Network, and PTL Network all went on the air via satellite. And local Christian stations were built in virtually every major market across America.

Once the interactive media of tomorrow has matured and produced its own class of prominent Christian personalities, their success will set the pace. The prominence of gospel broadcasters will peak, some will build great ministries, and the secular networks and stations will scratch their heads, the public will ask questions, and Christians will turn from simply *using* the new medium to *owning* it.

Phase 6: The medium slows. In the tradition of the marketplace, success also sows the seeds for the phase to follow. More gospel broadcasts means more competition for airtime and audiences, which means higher costs and less income, which means fewer prominent programs. As costs rise and viewership falls, broadcasters who built large organizations find their *ability* to raise funds can become a *need* to raise funds. Where the ministry once generated excitement to build new projects, now new projects generate excitement to sustain the ministry. Ultimately, the pressure becomes too much in a marketplace where competition for viewers drives up costs and fragments the market. At the same time, the position of Christian networks and stations is strengthened. They deliver consistent and responsive audiences—but at the potential cost of putting gospel programs in a "religious ghetto" seen only by Christians.

Servants God Can Use

Thus the interactive media of tomorrow can, if the past is prologue, be expected to: (1) grow quickly in a climate that favors innovative Christian broadcasters; (2) invite regulations, standards, and an economic rationale that favor professional operators; (3) give rise to national networks that offer new opportunities to carry gospel programs; (4) create prominent Christian media personalities; (5) inspire more gospel broadcasters to enter the medium; (6) meet the need for airtime and audiences through Christian-owned stations and networks; and (7) restrain the excesses of money and power through competition in the marketplace. At each phase, God can use all manner of servants to advance the cause of gospel broadcasting. From innovators to engineers, all will be needed. And from the past comes a picture of those servants God can use and the qualities he values in the field of religious broadcasting.

Servants of vision. When Paul Rader stood in a tiny makeshift booth on the roof of Chicago City Hall, with a telephone thrust through a cutout in the side, it wasn't very impressive. He thought "tabernaclism" was the way to evangelize the masses. But when response to the 1922 radio broadcast far surpassed his expectations, Rader was quick to see the vision. That same year, Walter Maier first saw a microphone at a Lutheran youth league conference, and soon the young seminary professor was single-handedly agitating for a radio station on campus. He saw the vision. In every religious media, in syndication and satellite and cable, it was men and women of vision who claimed them for Christ.

Servants of faith. What made Donald Grey Barnhouse sign a network contract for $40,000 when his own local program had finished the past year with only eleven cents? What made Walter Maier sit outside the CBS office, waiting patiently for an appointment, when he knew executives were opposed to paid religious programs? What made Billy Graham put out a shoebox in hopes of $25,000? What made Rex Humbard sign 101 stations when his financing was withdrawn? What made Pat Robertson leave his pastorate in New York to buy a run-down UHF station in Virginia? What made Harold Camping, a construction contractor, fund a radio station solely through listener support? Each time religious broadcasting has moved ahead, God has used those who were sensitive to his call, ready to step out in faith, to take risks, and to trust him for the result.

Servants of action. God uses believers not for their *ability* but for their *availability*. He uses people who are willing to take their orders and march forward. Though he has often raised up broadcasters who at first knew little about radio or television, God wills that his servants "press toward the mark." Henry Crowell kept WMBI on the air, launching a ministry God uses to this day, because he saw that mastering the new technical standards of 1927 was integral to his ministry. Over the years—1944, 1956, 1987—broadcasters have met each challenge by committing themselves anew to professional excellence. The Lord is honored when Christian broadcasters devote themselves to learn and practice the highest standards of both business and ministry.

Servants of heart. "What would you pay a man to raise $100 million a year? What's that worth?" With those words, uttered in a 1984 newspaper interview, Jim Bakker was saying, "God's work here can't go on without me. He needs me, I'm indispensable." Such pride declares, "I go first. I'm the one who counts around here." When the headlines tell of preachers who fall into sin, that's where it starts. No one person or organization is indispensable to God. If one falters, he can raise up another. Anyone can become a Jim Bakker but for daily submission to the Spirit of God. In the fishbowl of Christian media celebrity, pride is an easy snare. Throughout the history of religious broadcasting, God has used servants who put others first, who serve with compassionate hearts and a desire to proclaim the life-giving gospel of Christ to a lost and dying world.

Servants of the Book. When Charles Fuller was the largest broadcaster on network radio, spending $30,000 a week to air the *Old-Fashioned Revival Hour* on 465 stations across America, he was asked about his success. "I'm not interested in figures," he said. "I'm interested in souls. Some say I reach twenty million people. I don't know. All I know is that I preach the greatest message in the world. There may be greater orators, but nobody can preach a greater message, because I preach from the world's greatest Book. It is the old gospel, the simple gospel that pulls."

A generation later, Billy Graham was asked about his ministry. By the miracle of radio and television, his great crusades had reached audiences of multiplied millions. But the evangelist replied that he learned the secret before he ever stepped before a radio microphone or television camera. "I stopped trying to prove that the Bible was true. I had settled it in my own mind that it was, and this faith was conveyed to the audience. I found they were desperately hungry to hear what God had to say through his Holy Word. I began to rely upon Scripture itself, and God blessed."

To the listener, radio is only a disembodied voice. To the viewer, television is only noise and color. What allows radio and television to do the work of God? Not the sounds, not the pictures, not the camera angles or the technical wizardry. It is the Word of God, going out across the airwaves, that alone is "quick, and powerful, and sharper than any two-edged sword, piercing even to the dividing asunder of soul and spirit, . . . a discerner of the thoughts and intents of the heart. . . . So shall my word be that goeth forth out of my mouth; it shall not return unto me void, but it shall accomplish that which I please, and it shall prosper in the thing whereto I sent it" (Heb. 4:12; Isa. 55:11).

It was for that reason, and that reason alone, that a man in Omaha ran across town one day in 1923. He made it in time, red-faced and puffing, reaching the studio door just as Rev. R. R. Brown was preparing to leave. Brown had been invited to preach a Sunday sermon at the new radio station in town. He didn't believe it when they said his voice would be heard for hundreds of miles, had even wondered if he should accept the invitation at all. So he just offered a simple Bible message. That was all. But as he went to the door, the man from across town was waiting. He had heard the Word, knelt in his living room, and trusted Jesus Christ as his Savior. It was nothing, Brown realized, that he had done. His voice could barely be heard over the crackle of the man's crystal radio set. It was the Word, pure and simple. All because of the Word. "Hallelujah!" he shouted. "Unction can be transmitted!"

Appendix A

CHRONOLOGY OF RELIGIOUS BROADCASTING

Short History

When radio emerged as a public medium in the early 1920s, preachers were fascinated but cautious. Would it work? Would it last? Could a crackling, disembodied voice elicit response to the gospel? As one preacher asked, could unction be transmitted? At the time, great crusades in the mold of D. L. Moody and Billy Sunday, with dynamic preachers swaying vast crowds, were considered the modern method of mass evangelism. Yet as pioneers such as Paul Rader and R. R. Brown showed the effectiveness of radio evangelism, religious groups joined the general rush to claim a place in the fast-growing new medium.

By 1927 more than sixty religious groups, from individual churches to evangelistic organizations, had obtained licenses to operate radio stations. But radio was choking on its own growth. The airwaves were a bedlam. Stations would shift frequencies at will, change their hours of operation, alter the strength or direction of their signals. Public outcry prompted Congress in 1927 to establish the Federal Radio Commission to bring order out of chaos. The agency introduced technical standards that soon drove the cost and sophistication needed to run a radio station beyond the reach of most religious operators. Within six years the number of stations owned by religious groups was cut by more than half—to less than thirty.

But even as God closed the door on direct ownership of stations as the principal means of radio evangelism, he opened another. In 1927 two national radio networks, NBC and CBS, went on the air. A third network, the Mutual Broadcasting System (MBS), was formed in 1934. This development offered the way for a national gospel outreach that was not possible through small and scattered religious stations. Preachers could simply purchase airtime on these networks—a cost they recovered through listener donations—and were relieved of the burden of owning and operating a station. Men such as Walter Maier of *The Lutheran Hour* and Charles Fuller of *Old-Fashioned Revival Hour* built national network audiences in the millions.

The success of network radio evangelism brought two unintended results. Some unscrupulous racketeers entered radio to solicit funds and enrich themselves under the guise of religion. And the liberal church, led by the Federal (later National) Council of Churches, reacted against independent radio preachers who were not accountable to any denominational authority. They perceived the buying and selling of airtime for religious worship as a demeaning form of hucksterism.

From the beginning, the Federal Radio Commission (succeeded in 1934 by the Federal Communications Commission) viewed the airwaves as a public trust. To receive licenses, stations must pledge to serve the public interest—and religious programs were classed as a category that served the public. The Council of Churches argued that airtime for programs which were a public service should be donated by networks and stations. Airing religious programs *only* on a free or "sustaining" basis would also eliminate concerns about preachers soliciting funds over the air. Furthermore, as the representative body of American Protestantism, the Council would coordinate the distribution of radio time to ensure accountability.

NBC and CBS both adopted this policy. Since evangelicals could not purchase airtime, nor obtain sustaining time because they were not members of the theologically liberal Council of Churches, their voice was effectively cut off. Only the Mutual system, needing revenue as the newest network, would sell time for religious programs. By the early 1940s, however, as MBS gained enough advertising to do without revenue from the sale of time to gospel preachers, the network indicated it would curtail the practice. Evangelicals were independent by nature and their lack of a central organization now prevented any response. In 1942, however, the threat of being shut out from all three radio networks galvanized the movement into forming the National Association of Evangelicals. Yet because World War II affected every area of society, including the church, NAE was soon occupied by many vital issues other than broadcasting. Thus in 1944, with the sponsorship of NAE, radio preachers formed their own pressure group, National Religious Broadcasters (NRB), to deal specifically with broadcast issues.

Rather than risk an uncertain all-or-nothing fight for congressional legislation on First Amendment grounds, or litigation that would alienate the networks, NRB decided to emphasize education and voluntary self-regulation. The group adopted a code of ethics and worked to show network executives that evangelical broadcasters could be responsible if given the opportunity to purchase airtime. NRB explained the place of evangelicals in the Protestant church and why sustaining-time policies unfairly excluded them. The strategy bore fruit in 1949 when the ABC network, formed four years earlier, reversed its ban on selling time for religious programs. The other networks eventually followed.

In the years ahead, though networks would revise their policies from time to time, the consensus generally shifted to the NRB position.

During the 1950s, two important developments occurred in religious broadcasting. First, as radio licensing boomed after World War II, evangelicals began returning to direct ownership of stations—but with a difference. Some Christian stations were now run on a commercial basis. They made a profit from selling airtime to preachers, who were in turn glad to get a dependable radio outlet. Also, broadcasters discovered that radio *stations*, and not just radio *programs*, could be sustained on the basis of listener support. The second development of the decade was the advent of gospel television. Utilizing this medium was left to a new generation of preachers, men such as Rex Humbard, Oral Roberts, and Jerry Falwell, since the styles and formats of radio evangelists did not transfer effectively to television.

After their early success, NRB members grew complacent. In 1956 the National Council of Churches moved into the gap, using the issue of television to renew its arguments against paid religious programs. The threat reenergized NRB and the challenge was decisively beaten back. The victory was fairly won in 1960, when the FCC ruled that stations could count paid religious broadcasts toward their public service requirements. From then on, stations could sell the time they once had donated—and did. Gospel broadcasting mushroomed, growing into a large industry during the 1960s and 1970s.

The invention of videotape, which allowed easy duplication of programs for mass distribution to stations, vastly enlarged the number of outlets that could carry evangelical broadcasts. By the late 1970s, Jerry Falwell was the largest syndicator, secular or religious, on network television. Rex Humbard amassed the largest independent network of stations in the world. *Oral Roberts and You* was the highest rated religious hour in America. Sustaining time, which accounted for 47 percent of religious broadcasts in 1959, faded by 1977 to only 8 percent. When the National Council of Churches endorsed paid programs in 1978, the last obstacle seemed clear. Religious cable television developed during the 1970s, and in 1977–78 three national Christian television networks began transmitting programs by satellite. At the same time, the FCC authorized the use of inexpensive earth translators. Broadcasters could feed Christian radio and television programs to towns and rural areas via a $40,000 translator, rather than spending millions to build a full-fledged station.

However, one more obstacle remained. Religious broadcasting would have to survive its own success. As the industry gained in influence and power, prominent broadcasters sought to use their medium not only to proclaim the gospel. Christian media now had the potential to bind evangelicals into a cohesive social movement, a force for restoring a moral, social, and political climate in which the Christian message could prosper. Presidents Ford, Carter, Reagan, and Bush were regular visitors to NRB conventions as the power of evangelical voters gained recognition. One broadcaster, Jerry Falwell, founded a potent "Moral Majority" political movement in 1979. Another broadcaster, Pat Robertson, made a serious run for president in 1987–88.

Perhaps inevitably, though, power paved the way for corruption. Those who had built large ministries now faced the financial pressure of maintaining them, constantly seeking new ways to motivate viewer support. When prominent broadcasters Jim Bakker and Jimmy Swaggart were embroiled in a series of sensational financial and sexual scandals during 1987–89, all religious broadcasters were tarnished. Because their growth had invited scrutiny, the public was already wary of the lifestyles and political motives of televangelists. Now their distrust hit new heights. Donations to all ministries declined. Yet lawmakers and the public did not question the *right* of independent preachers to use the airwaves, as they had fifty years ago, but only the *responsibilities*. Though congressional hearings were held in 1988, the chief outcome was an IRS policy to work more closely with individual broadcasters in assuring compliance with tax-exemption rules.

Today the religious broadcasting industry is emerging from a period of self-correction. Events have heightened the sensitivity of broadcasters to public concerns. In 1988, formation of the NRB Ethics and Financial Integrity Commission (EFICOM) introduced, for the first time, standards that could be objectively measured for compliance. However, market forces are also playing a corrective role. The success of television preachers inspired others to enter the medium, increasing demand for religious airtime and driving up its cost, while also boosting competition for listener support. As a result, evangelical syndicators have faded from the high-profile scene of network television. Instead, they have moved to religious cable and satellite networks that deliver consistent audiences or have taken their programs to the lower cost medium of radio. And as the focus of religious broadcasting moves from *programs* to *networks*, the emphasis is shifting from individual personalities to corporate structures.

Through cable and satellite technology, Christian media today enjoys more coverage than ever before. But this same technology, by giving audiences vastly expanded choices, has fragmented the viewing public into small niches based upon individual interests. As syndication gives way to Christian networks, broadcasters face the potential of being relegated to a "religious channel ghetto" seen only by Christians. Their challenge is to find ways of using the media technologies now being developed to meet viewer needs and reach out to the broader public.

1920 (Nov. 2): First regular broadcast station. KDKA/Pittsburgh becomes the first to begin regularly scheduled broadcasting, commencing with coverage of the Harding-Cox presidential election.

1921 (Jan. 2): First religious broadcast. KDKA airs the Sunday vespers service of Pittsburgh's Calvary Episcopal Church, presided over by junior associate Rev. Lewis Whittemore.

1921 (Sept. 15): First station license. The federal Department of Commerce awards the first broadcast license to WBZ of Springfield (later Boston), Massachusetts.

1921 (Nov. 27): First continuous religious program. Broadcasts begin in New York by the Radio Church of America.

1921 (Dec. 22): First religious station. Church of the Covenant (now National Presbyterian Church), a congregation in Washington, D.C., receives the first broadcast license issued to a religious organization.

1922: First religious broadcaster. Paul Rader is invited by the mayor of Chicago to give a radio address from City Hall, and when response far surpasses expectations, Rader begins a radio ministry.

1922 (Aug. 28): First radio advertising. An economic basis for the new medium is discovered, when a New York City real estate firm sells two buildings after sponsoring a program on station WEAF in exchange for a broadcast announcement that the properties are for sale.

1923 (April 8): First radio church. R. R. Brown begins radio broadcasting and later realizes his *Radio Chapel Service* audience is really a new form of the church. Rather than simply preaching to listeners, Brown recruits them into an organization, the World Radio Congregation, so they can be mobilized for prayer and charitable work.

1924 (Feb. 6): KFSG begins operation. Founded by Aimee Semple MacPherson's International Church of the Foursquare Gospel, KFSG/Los Angeles signs on the air with the words of John 3:16.

1924: KFUO begins operation. Walter Maier, an Old Testament professor at Concordia Seminary in St. Louis, begins his broadcasting career by convincing the school to operate a radio station.

1926 (July 28): WMBI begins operation. Led at first by program manager Wendell Loveless and station manager Henry Crowell, over the years the station becomes a training ground for many important evangelical broadcasters.

1927: Federal Radio Commission formed. Under the Radio Act of 1927, the agency is created to bring order out of chaos on the unregulated airwaves. By introducing technical standards and favoring commercial stations, the FRC puts most religious stations out of business. Between 1927 and 1933 the number of stations owned by churches and religious groups declines from sixty-three to thirty. Most of these stations are small and broadcast only a few hours on Sunday. As a result, they cannot afford or justify the professional operation that FRC licensing standards require. The development marks the end of direct ownership of stations as the principal means for religious broadcasting, at least until after World War II.

1927: CBS and NBC networks formed. Long-distance lines needed for network broadcasting are controlled by the American Telephone and Telegraph Company, which also owns many radio stations. Only AT&T stations can use the lines, until 1926 when the company sells the stations to the Radio Corporation of America. RCA forms the National Broadcasting Company (NBC), which begins network operation with a New Year's Day 1927 broadcast of the Rose Bowl football game. Later that year the Columbia Broadcasting System (CBS) is also formed. Thus, as the door shuts for religious broadcasters on direct ownership of stations, network radio opens an opportunity for even greater gospel outreach.

1927: First woman broadcaster. Lois Crawford of religious station KFGQ in Boone, Iowa, receives the first operators license issued by the Federal Radio Commission to a woman.

1928: First network religious program. Donald Grey Barnhouse, pastor of Tenth Presbyterian Church in Philadelphia, becomes the first to purchase network airtime for a religious program. The year before, he broadcast a local program and finished 1927 with a balance of eleven cents but nevertheless signs a $40,000 contract with CBS.

1928: First religious studio broadcast. NBC airs *National Radio Pulpit*, sponsored by the Federal (later National) Council of

Churches with speaker S. Parkes Cadman, the first religious program broadcast from a network studio.

1928: NBC bans paid time. With *National Radio Pulpit*, NBC and the Council of Churches agree that airtime should not be sold but only donated by the network for religious programs.

1930: First television station. W2XBS New York, an NBC affiliate, becomes the first commercial television station to go on the air with regular broadcasts.

1930 (Oct. 2): Maier goes national. *The Lutheran Hour* airs on network radio for the first time, eventually becoming the largest radio venture of its day. By the 1940s the program is heard in thirty-six languages over twelve hundred stations with an estimated worldwide audience of nearly seven hundred million. When Maier dies in 1950 at the age of fifty-six, he is believed to have preached the gospel to more people than any man in history.

1931 (Feb. 22): First international religious station. Radio Vatican goes on the air from Vatican City, beaming religious services across Europe with a 10,000-watt transmitter.

1931: CBS bans paid time. In response to controversy over the politicized radio sermons of Father Charles Coughlin, CBS decides to produce its own religious programs in cooperation with the Council of Churches, rather than sell airtime to religious broadcasters.

1931 (Dec. 25): First missionary radio station. HCJB, "The Voice of the Andes," begins broadcasting from Quito, Ecuador. The founders are Clarence Jones, a protégé of Paul Rader, and Reuben Larson, who committed his life to missionary radio after hearing a challenge by R. R. Brown.

1934 (July 11): Federal Communications Commission formed. After passage on June 19 of the Communications Act of 1934, the FCC is established as a permanent agency to replace the Federal Radio Commission, which had to be reauthorized on an annual basis.

1934: Mutual Network formed. The Mutual Broadcasting System becomes the first viable competition for NBC and CBS, and sells time to evangelical broadcasters as a way to raise the revenues it needs to get established in the marketplace. By contrast, the older networks do not sell airtime but provide free or "sustaining" time to be distributed to Protestant broadcasters by the liberal Federal Council of Churches. As a result, evangelicals are shut off from NBC and CBS.

1934: Federal Council allocates time. The Federal Council of Churches forms a department that assumes responsibility for allocating sustaining time on network radio, taking over from the Greater New York Council of Churches.

1936: First (?) Black religious broadcaster. Reverend Clayton Russell begins regular broadcasting of church services on KFOX/Los Angeles.

1937: Fuller goes national. Charles Fuller brings his local program onto the Mutual network. Soon the *Old-Fashioned Revival Hour* is the top religious broadcast in America, with an estimated audience of ten million. In 1939 he introduces a second one-hour network program, and by 1943 Fuller's Gospel Broadcasting Association is the top broadcaster on the Mutual system, spending 50 percent more money for airtime than the network's next-largest secular customer.

1939: Roosevelt television broadcast. When President Franklin Roosevelt opens the 1939 New York World's Fair via television, the broadcast generates intense public excitement in the new medium. Applications for television licenses pour into the FCC.

1940: First religious telecast. The Easter Sunday service of a local church is telecast over W2XBS/New York.

1941: Television advertising approved. The FCC gives limited permission to allow commercial advertising on television, thus assuring an economic basis for the new medium.

1942: FCC freezes radio. With America's recent entry into World War II, all radio communications are brought under the Defense Communications Board. Soon afterward the FCC freezes all radio assignments and places a ban on new station construction.

1942 (April 7): NAE organized. As radio preachers become more prominent, the Federal Council of Churches steps up efforts to stop networks and individual stations from selling airtime to religious broadcasters. Since NBC and CBS have always followed this policy, the Mutual System is targeted. Galvanized by the threat of being cut off from all three major networks, conservatives meet in St. Louis to form the National Association of Evangelicals.

1943: Mutual announces restrictions. In the fall of the year, MBS announces its intention to severely curtail its practice of selling time for religious programs by the 1944 season. The development sets off a firestorm in the evangelical community, which is also worried that individual stations will follow suit.

1944 (April 12): NRB organized. Even as the threat to gospel broadcasting deepens, the new NAE is increasingly occupied in many other vital wartime areas where a united evangelical voice is needed. Broadcasters decide they need to organize themselves into an effective pressure group that deals officially with radio issues. With the support of NAE and in conjunction with its second annual convention in Columbus, Ohio, National Religious Broadcasters is organized. An NRB constitutional convention is called in Chicago for September 21, 1944, at which time the new association is incorporated.

1944: Fuller books independent network. Forced by Mutual to cut back from two one-hour programs to a single half-hour weekly broadcast, Charles Fuller assembles a national network of independent radio stations to carry his *Old-Fashioned Revival Hour.* This innovation sets a model that remains dominant in religious broadcasting through today.

1945: ABC network formed. In 1927, when it added the former AT&T stations to its existing operations, NBC formed a "Red" and a "Blue" network. In 1945, the government forces NBC to divest itself, and the company sells its "Blue" network to the American Broadcasting Company. The new ABC network adopts the policy of only airing religious programs on sustaining time.

1945: Postwar license boom. As the war draws to a close, the FCC lifts its radio freeze and, by the end of the year, issues more than a thousand station licenses. As a result, noncommercial stations begin returning to the market for the first time since the late 1920s. The move also allows FM stations, which had first been licensed in 1941 until frozen the next year, to become a factor in the market.

1945: Federal Council creates film unit. The Protestant Film Commission is formed by the Federal Council of Churches to coordinate film production among its member denominations. In 1950 the unit merges with the radio department to become the Broadcasting and Film Commission of the newly formed National Council of Churches.

1946: First commercial religious station. Started by brothers David and Egon Hofer, KRDU in Dinuba, California, is believed to be the first Christian radio station run as a commercial enterprise. The station generates revenues by selling airtime to gospel broadcasters, who in turn are glad to have a dependable radio outlet without the restrictions of secular stations. They also benefit by placing their programs on a station that attracts listeners with an interest in religion.

1947: FCC issues television standards. The agency adopts standard specifications for television receivers, setting off a boom in the sale of TV sets that assures an audience for broadcasters.

1948 (Jan. 1): First "made for TV" worship service. Since the first weekly broadcast of *The Lutheran Hour* for 1948 falls on New Year's Day, Walter Maier has the program telecast over KSD-TV/St. Louis.

1948 (June 4): FEBC begins operation. The Far East Broadcasting Company brings missionary radio to Asia when broadcasts begin from its station in Manila, Philippines. Founders are Robert Bowman, John Broger, and William Roberts.

1948: First campus station. John Brown University of Siloam Springs, Arkansas, a Christian college, establishes the first narrowcast radio station on any religious or secular campus in America.

1949: KTIS begins operation. Owned by Northwestern Schools (later College) of Minneapolis, Minnesota, KTIS is the first station in what later becomes an important Christian radio network.

1949: ABC reverses ban. The efforts of NRB pay off as ABC becomes the first network to reverse its ban on selling airtime to religious broadcasters.

1949: Network television emerges. The development of coaxial cables during 1949–51 makes network television feasible.

1949: First evangelical on network TV. Percy Crawford becomes the first gospel broadcaster to appear on network television, coast to coast. *Youth on the March* is seen in a dozen markets nationwide, continuing on ABC until 1951.

1950 (Jan. 11): Walter Maier dies. Only fifty-six, Maier had achieved a public stature that was only matched in a later day by Billy Graham. His loss stuns the evangelical community, for Maier's sterling public reputation set a positive tone that benefited all gospel broadcasters.

1950 (Nov. 5): Graham goes on radio and TV. The *Hour of Decision* radio program is inaugurated as the Billy Graham Atlanta Crusade is carried over 150 stations on the ABC radio network. This and other Graham crusades are also captured on film, to be made later into motion pictures and into a series of *Hour of Decision* telecasts that appear from 1950 to 1954.

1951–56: Religious television pioneers. Names that later become synonymous with religious television first appear on the air, including Bishop Fulton Sheen (1951), Rex Humbard (1953), Oral Roberts (1954), and Jerry Falwell (1956).

1951 (Oct. 1): First husband-wife team. Norman Vincent and Ruth Peale become the first husband-and-wife team to host a religious program.

1954 (Feb. 22): Voice of Tangier begins operation. Missionary radio comes to Europe and North Africa from "The Voice of Tangier" station built in Tangier, Morocco, by Paul Freed. The ministry later develops into today's Trans World Radio.

1954: Television surpasses radio. For the first time, television industry revenues surpass those of radio.

1954–60: Christian radio networks form. Christian broadcasters begin group ownership of multiple stations. Among those who started with one station and now begin acquiring additional outlets are Moody Bible Institute, Northwestern College, John Brown University, and the Pillar of Fire denomination.

1956: Another Council clash. The National (formerly Federal) Council of Churches uses the growth of television to renew the debate over paid versus sustaining time. Since many religious programs are of poor technical quality, the Council also proposes all Protestant broadcasts be produced through its film department. The move is defeated as secular broadcasters generally take the side of NRB, seeing the issue in terms of broadcast freedom.

1956–57: Networks reverse ban. NBC and CBS reverse their bans on selling time to religious broadcasters, joining ABC, which made the change in 1949. Though the networks would often revise their policies, from this time the industry generally shifts toward the NRB position.

1957 (June 1): First television crusade. The Billy Graham New York Crusade becomes the first nationally televised crusade ever seen in America. The event is filmed for a series of seventeen weekly broadcasts. More than 1.5 million letters are received by the Graham ministry, and some 330,000 viewers write to share their decisions for Christ.

1959 (Feb. 4): First listener-supported station. Radio programs had long been supported by listeners. And though stations had been underwritten before by donations, these funds were raised with denominational or institutional backing. Under Harold Camping, Family Radio of San Francisco (later Oakland), California, becomes what is believed to be the first unaffiliated Christian station operated solely through listener support.

1960: FCC rules on public interest. The agency declares that stations may count paid religious programs, and not just sustaining time broadcasts, toward their license requirements to provide public interest programming. Now, as stations can sell time they once donated, the sale of airtime for gospel programs begins to boom.

1960 (July 17): First Christian-owned TV station. WPCA/Philadelphia goes on the air, purchased by evangelist Percy Crawford, the first gospel broadcaster to own a television station. Though WPCA airs Christian programming, it is a local network affiliate and not licensed as an expressly religious station. After Crawford's untimely death in October 1960, the station ultimately fails.

1960 (Oct. 16): Trans World Radio begins operation. When its station in Tangier is nationalized by a newly independent Moroccan government, a new site is secured on the European mainland at Monte Carlo, Monaco. Renamed "Trans World Radio," the ministry grows in time to become the world's largest missionary radio network.

1961 (Oct. 1): First religious TV station. Founded by former pastor Pat Robertson under the name Christian Broadcasting Network, WYAH-TV goes on the air from Portsmouth, Virginia, with a mix of religious and secular programs.

1964: UHF reception mandated. Congress makes the UHF band a practical reality by enacting a law that requires all television sets to be manufactured for both VHF and UHF reception. The addition of seventy new channels opens opportunities for gospel broadcasters.

1966: First Christian talk show. Hosted by Pat Robertson on WYAH-TV, the success of the *700 Club* annual telethon leads to a daily talk show program of the same name, the first time such a program format is attempted on religious television.

1968: First all-religious TV station. The first exclusively religious television station is licensed to the Faith Broadcasting Network, founded by the Faith Center Church of Glendale, California, and its pastor, Gene Scott.

1968: First "alternative" TV station. Evangelist Lester Sumrall and his LeSea Broadcasting Company purchase a defunct Indianapolis station and introduce the concept of family-oriented entertainment, rather than strictly religious programs, as an alternative to secular television offerings.

1968–70: Religious syndication pioneers. Christian broadcasters go into national syndication, assembling independent television networks by purchasing time on local stations around the United States. Three preachers, who will come to dominate religious syndication over the next decade, enter national television ministry at this time—Rex Humbard (1968), Oral Roberts (1969), and Jerry Falwell (1970).

1971: First religious cable channel. The station operated by Redwood Community Chapel in Castro Valley, California, becomes the first religious station to be offered over a local cable television system.

1971: First religious satellite broadcast. Proceedings of the annual NRB convention are broadcast from Washington via Intelsat IV satellite to the Trans World Radio station at Bonaire, Netherlands Antilles, for shortwave retransmission to South America and Europe.

1975–76: Presidential power. On January 28, 1975, Gerald Ford becomes the first United States president to address an NRB convention. Ford returns at his own request the following year, and his February 22, 1976, address is a turning point in awakening religious broadcasters to their potential as a social and political force. In 1976, NRB representatives are twice invited to the White House. The association conducts interviews for distribution to the Christian media with both major 1976 presidential candidates, Republican Gerald Ford and Democrat Jimmy Carter. For the first time in the modern political era, candidates are invited to describe their personal religious faith and how it influences their decisions. Both Ford and Carter profess a born-again Christian faith. The evangelical vote is later cited as a contributor to the Carter electoral victory.

1977 (April): First Christian satellite operator. The Christian Broadcasting Network becomes the first U.S. religious organization licensed to operate a satellite earth station. CBN is followed in May 1977 by the Trinity Broadcasting Network, founded by Paul Crouch, and in 1978 by PTL Television and LeSea Broadcasting.

1977 (May 1): First live satellite telecast. Hosted by Paul and Jan Crouch, the Trinity Broadcasting Network beams its *Praise the Lord* program, live via satellite from the Mount of Olives in Jerusalem, to viewers of the local TBN station in Southern California.

1977 (May 15): First 24-hour Christian station. KBTN-TV, the Los Angeles area outlet owned by Trinity Broadcasting Network, becomes the first station to adopt a twenty-four-hour exclusively religious broadcast schedule.

1977: Dobson on the air. Psychologist James Dobson debuts *Focus on the Family* on local radio, and within fifteen years it becomes the largest Christian radio venture of all time with four thousand outlets worldwide.

1978: Council endorses paid time. The National Council of Churches reverses its longtime position and endorses the sale of airtime for religious programs. Between 1959 and 1979, sustaining time had declined from 47 to 8 percent of all religious broadcasts.

1978: Black religious broadcasting. The nation's first Black-owned religious radio station, WYIS/Philadelphia, goes on the air. The outlet is headed by B. Samuel Hart, speaker on *The Grand Old Gospel Hour* heard on some 130 stations in the United States and five countries. In Detroit, WGPR becomes America's first Black-owned television station, airing a religious format. Black broadcasters organize their first "strategy conference" under the banner of the four-year-old NRB Ethnic Broadcasters Committee, later renamed (under NRB auspices) Black National Religious Broadcasters.

1978–80: Religious syndicators are largest. By the end of the 1970s, Jerry Falwell is the most syndicated broadcaster—secular or religious—in the United States. Rex Humbard purchases time on the largest independent television network in the world. And Oral Roberts enjoys the most watched religious program in America.

1978 (Jan.): FCC okays translators. The agency rules that translators, equipment often placed in rural areas to pick up broadcast signals for local viewing, may be fed by satellite. With this action, Christian radio and television can now be extended to communities that cannot support a full broadcast station of their own. Translators cost forty thousand dollars, compared to more than millions of dollars to construct a full-fledged television or radio station.

1978: Controversy mobilizes evangelicals. The Internal Revenue Service, under the direction of the Carter administration, proposes that most Christian schools be *assumed* guilty of racial discrimination—and stripped of their tax-exempt status—unless they can prove otherwise. The evangelical community erupts, and for the first time, the religious media plays the decisive role in mobilizing born-again Christians for political action.

1979: Moral Majority formed. Concerned about the liberal drift of the Carter administration, NRB invites prominent gospel broadcasters to meet and discuss their role in educating Christians about the political process. Jerry Falwell organizes the Moral Majority and Pat Robertson forms the Freedom Council. Both groups play major roles in mobilizing Christians during the 1980s.

1980: Political decisions. After President Carter addresses the NRB convention the night before, NRB leaders are invited for a White House breakfast on January 22. The session produces little agreement on political issues, though the president is undeniably a man of like born-again faith. As a result, broadcasters begin placing more emphasis on candidates' public positions rather than personal faith. On April 29, nearly half a million Christians assemble on the National Mall at a "Washington for Jesus" rally, perhaps the largest gathering ever in Washington. In August, broadcasters mobilize more than fifteen thousand pastors to attend a National Affairs Briefing—at which Republican presidential candidate Ronald Reagan unofficially wins the hearts of delegates. NRB sponsors news conferences for the Christian media with Reagan and independent candidate John Anderson, but is snubbed by the Carter campaign. On election day, evangelical voters switch en masse to the Republican column.

1981: Hispanic religious broadcasting. As the Hispanic population of the United States grows, Spanish language programs become an increasingly vital aspect of gospel radio and television. Under the sponsorship of NRB, broadcasters band together and form Hispanic National Religious Broadcasters (HNRB).

1984 (April 16): Annenberg Study released. With bipartisan support from both NRB and the National Council of Churches, a study of religious broadcasting is undertaken by the Annenberg School of Communication of the University of Pennsylvania. Titled *Religion and Television*, this major study receives wide attention in the secular news media, as the report denies the charge that TV preachers "steal" attendance and donations away from local churches.

1985: Humbard off the air. After thirty-three years on television, Rex Humbard ends his program. His previous success inspired others to enter the medium, thus increasing competition for airtime and viewer support. As a result, his program revenues cannot keep up with rising costs. Humbard also cites constant pressure on broadcasters to fund highly visible building projects that generate continued viewer excitement and financial support. The cancellation marks a trend away from program syndication as the focus of religious broadcasting and toward an emphasis on Christian networks and stations able to deliver a consistent audience.

1985: First Christian radio news network. Christian broadcaster Marlin Maddoux launches USA Radio as "the first conservative news radio network," and in less than a decade the twenty-four-hour satellite service is carried by more than one thousand affiliates, most of them secular outlets.

1986–88: Robertson for president. The growth of religious broadcasting seems to reach its logical conclusion as one of the industry's own, Pat Robertson, mounts a campaign for president of the United States. Despite early success, Robertson ultimately bows to George Bush, the eventual Republican nominee and presidential winner.

1987 (Jan. 4): Oral Roberts questioned. Prominent television preacher Oral Roberts announces God will "take me home" unless his supporters send $8 million by the end of March 1987. The ultimatum touches off a national wave of ridicule and indignation.

1987 (March 19): Bakker resigns PTL. Amid explosive allegations of sexual misconduct and countercharges of blackmail and extortion, televangelist Jim Bakker resigns as head of a mammoth ministry that includes the PTL television network and Heritage USA theme park. Soon the unfolding scandal is fanned by findings of gross financial mismanagement and fraud. Given the spectacular growth of religious broadcasting, an abuse of this kind was perhaps inevitable. But the PTL scandal plunges the industry into the second great crisis of its history (after the battle over paid versus sustaining time). NRB ultimately fends off calls for legislated restrictions on gospel broadcasters, yet the task of restoring public confidence continues.

1988: EFICOM established. With the growth of the industry, the increased potential for abuse becomes apparent to NRB leaders. In 1978 the association toughens its code of ethics, and a year later endorses the newly formed Evangelical Council for Financial Accountability (ECFA). In 1986, before the PTL scandal, NRB begins the process of forming its own Ethics and Financial Integrity Commission to enforce objectively measurable standards of compliance. EFICOM is formally approved by the NRB membership and, under the administration of ECFA, begins operation in early 1988. After five years, ECFA grows large enough to take over the functions of EFICOM.

1990: Digital HDTV. The General Instrument Corporation bypasses a Japanese "analog" technique to develop a digital system for high definition television (HDTV). Since computers employ the same digital system for processing information, the breakthrough promises an eventual merging of video and computing into a single interactive medium in which users can both receive and transmit through television.

1993: Media "merger mania." In response to an FCC competition, contestants pool their four rival plans into a single proposed industry standard for HDTV. The system would allow television sets to receive and display both video and computing signals, a first step toward an interactive medium. The General Instrument, and Microsoft corporations announce a joint effort to develop a remote control unit—really a handheld personal computer—to accommodate interactive television. After intense speculation about a war to wire the "information highway," the telephone and cable television industries rush to become partners rather than rivals. By the end of the year, no less than five mergers are announced between major telephone and cable operators. The action is paced by the nation's two largest cable companies, Tele-Communications, Inc. (TCI), and Time Warner, who team up with Bell Atlantic and U.S. West, respectively. (The Bell/TCI merger, however, is later called off.)

1993: Wireless advances. Among the year's mergers, AT&T announces it will acquire Macaw Cellular, a leader in cellular technology, to position itself for the coming of wireless communications. In 1993, technical advances in signal compression allow the first practical application of direct broadcast satellite (DBS) television, which the FCC had first approved in 1982. Two DBS services, DirecTV (owned by General Motors' Hughes Electronics) and USSB (Hubbard Broadcasting), are introduced. The systems allow homeowners to receive more than 150 channels via satellite dishes only eighteen inches wide.

1993: First interactive Christian media. The New Inspirational Network, purchased by evangelist Morris Cerullo from the former PTL operation bankrupted by Jim Bakker, announces plans to begin a Christian home shopping club over its cable channel that reaches more than seven million homes.

Appendix B

BIOGRAPHIES OF RELIGIOUS BROADCASTERS

The story of Christian broadcasting is best seen through the faithful and colorful men and women who made its history. Because this book is organized chronologically and not topically, however, the narrative cannot wholly describe the careers of the broadcasters you have met in these pages. Each personality enters the story at a time when his or her contribution is most vital, and then the story moves on. To tell "whatever became of" any individual is beyond the scope of this volume. Instead, a brief biography is offered below about the personalities presented in this book, and other important broadcasters who could only be mentioned in passing. If you are interested in more information about their careers, contact National Religious Broadcasters.

Ben Armstrong. After his graduation from New York University—from which he would later earn a master's degree (1950) and a doctorate (1967)—Armstrong was ordained in 1949 by the United Presbyterian Church and served pastorates in New York and New Jersey. In 1958 Armstrong joined Trans World Radio, founded by brother-in-law Paul Freed, before his 1967 appointment as executive secretary (later executive director) of National Religious Broadcasters. Beginning with an annual budget of only nine thousand dollars, during twenty-three years at the NRB post he helped bring the organization to a position of preeminence in the Christian broadcasting industry.

William Ward Ayer. Born in 1892 in Shediac, New Brunswick, Canada, Ayer ran away from home in the years after his mother died in 1897. He gave his life to Christ at a 1916 Billy Sunday revival meeting in Boston, then attended Moody Bible Institute in Chicago. After graduation in 1919, Ayer went on to pastor Baptist churches in Illinois, Indiana, and Ontario, before moving to Calvary Baptist Church in New York City where he presided over one of the leading fundamentalist congregations in America. During his tenure (1936–49), Ayer saw membership grow from four hundred to sixteen hundred, and recorded more than five thousand conversions. His media ventures included *Calvary Pulpit* magazine, ten published books, and a weekly radio program over WHN/New York (later WMGM/New York) with an estimated 250,000 listeners. In 1944 Ayer was elected the first president of National Religious Broadcasters and drafted its Code of Ethics. When he departed Calvary in 1949, and until his death in 1985, Ayer continued an independent radio ministry and traveled extensively as a Bible conference speaker.

Donald Grey Barnhouse. Born in 1895 in Watsonville, California, Barnhouse was raised in a devout Methodist home. At age seventeen he enrolled in the Bible Institute of Los Angeles, then attended the University of Chicago and Princeton Theological Seminary, until joining the Army Signal Corps in 1917. After the war Barnhouse stayed six years in Europe, first as a missionary in Belgium (1919–21), then as a Reformed pastor in the French Alps. He returned in 1925 to the United States and settled in Philadelphia, where he served at Grace Presbyterian (1925–27) and Tenth Presbyterian churches until his death in 1960. From that base, Barnhouse began the first network radio ministry in 1928; published *Revelation* magazine (later *Eternity*); published a dozen books; and traveled worldwide as a Bible conference speaker. In 1949 he was among the first to switch from an evangelistic radio format to an emphasis on equipping Christians for ministry. The *Bible Study Hour* broadcast continues today under James Montgomery Boice.

Eugene Bertermann. Born in 1914 in Bittern Lake, Alberta, Canada, the son of a Lutheran pastor, Bertermann entered Concordia College of St. Louis at age fifteen. He studied at the Lutheran Church Missouri Synod (LCMS) institution for eight years, earning a bachelor's degree (1937) before going on to master's (1938) and doctoral (1940) degrees at Washington University, and LCMS ordination in 1940. While receiving a Lutheran Laymen's League scholarship at Concordia, the organization put Bertermann to work answering mail for its *Lutheran Hour* radio program, broadcast by Concordia professor Walter Maier. He was associated with that ministry for the next twenty-four years, and as business manager saw the broadcast grow to 1330 stations in more than seventy nations. After leaving *The Lutheran Hour* in 1959, Bertermann went on to serve as executive director of the LCMS television department (1959–67), Lutheran Laymen's League (1967–71), and Far East Broadcasting Company (1971–78). From 1978 until his death in 1984, he was associate director of Lutheran Bible Translators, a missionary work he helped found in 1964. Bertermann was also the longest-serving NRB president in its history, having held the office from 1957 to 1975.

Robert Bowman. After graduating from Southern California Bible College in 1934, Bowman joined the *Haven of Rest* radio ministry of Paul Myers in Los Angeles. After seeing the many letters and testimonies of listeners who came to Christ through the broadcast, he gained a vision for using radio to reach other nations, particularly the Far East. That vision was shared by an old Bible school classmate, John Broger, then on wartime duty with the U.S. Navy in the Pacific. When Broger was discharged in 1946, he teamed with Bowman and a local pastor, William Roberts, to scrape up one thousand dollars and form the Far East Broadcasting Company (FEBC). After scouting sites unsuccessfully in China and taking ship for home, Broger chanced upon a property in Manila, Philippines, and in 1948 a radio station was built on the site. Bowman continues to serve today with FEBC, now headquartered in La Mirada, California. Under his leadership the ministry has grown to some thirty stations worldwide, broadcasting to Asia and Latin America in more than one hundred languages and dialects, and is heard in more than one hundred nations with two-thirds of the world's population.

Myron Boyd. When his denomination launched a national radio program in 1945 and chose Boyd as its speaker, he had already been broadcasting for nine years as pastor of Seattle's First Free Methodist Church. In 1947, Boyd resigned both the pulpit and his local weekly program, as the *Light and Life Hour* prospered and claimed his energies. He remained twenty years in the post, building the broadcast into an outreach heard in seventy nations, resigning as speaker in 1965 after his election as bishop (one of six) for the denomination. Boyd retired in 1976 and died two years later at the age of seventy.

R. R. Brown. Born in 1885 in Dagus Mines, Pennsylvania, Brown was educated at the Missionary Training Institute (now Nyack College) and pastored Christian and Missionary Alliance (CMA) churches in Beaver Falls, Pennsylvania, Chicago, and

Omaha, Nebraska, where in 1923 he founded the Omaha Gospel Tabernacle. That same year he began preaching over the radio, ultimately reaching an audience of half a million across the Midwest. Listeners were invited to join the "World Radio Congregation," an innovation now seen as the first time radio was viewed as a separate form of the church. Brown continued broadcasting until his death in 1964, at which time his *Radio Chapel Service* was the longest running religious program in the world (and was continued by his church until 1977). Brown served on the CMA Board of Managers from 1925 to 1960, and in 1935 founded the Bible and Missionary Conference Center in Okoboji Lakes, Iowa.

Robert Cook. Born in 1912 in Cleveland, Cook attended Moody Bible Institute, Wheaton College, and Eastern Baptist Seminary, and was ordained a Baptist minister in 1935. He pastored churches in Philadelphia and Chicago before becoming cofounder and president (1948–57) of Youth for Christ International, and vice president (1957–62) of Scripture Press. His radio career began in 1962 when Cook was named president of The King's College, founded in Briarcliff, New York, by evangelist and broadcaster Percy Crawford. As speaker for the college's radio outreach, *The King's Hour*, he became a leading national voice for the gospel. Even after his 1985 retirement as president, Cook continued to represent the college as its broadcast speaker until his death in 1991. A prolific writer, Cook authored nine books including *Now That I Believe*, a million-copy bestseller that has been translated into nearly thirty languages. He was NRB president from 1985 to 1988.

Lois Crawford. Born in 1892 in Boone, Iowa, Crawford was associated her entire life with the work founded by her father in 1891. In 1927 the elder Crawford purchased a 10-watt transmitter. That year, when the Federal Radio Commission ruled stations must have professional operators, Lois Crawford became the first woman in America to earn a First Class Radio Telephone License.

Ordained by her father in 1923, she succeeded him as president of Boone Biblical Ministries and pastor of Boone Biblical Church after his death in 1936. Crawford served as ministry president for fifty years, until her own death in 1986, supervising a Christian day school (K–12) and a two-year Bible college, youth camp, children's home, retirement home, religious bookstore, and radio station KFGQ-AM-FM.

Percy Crawford. Born in 1902 in Minnedosa, Manitoba, Canada, Crawford was educated at the Bible Institute of Los Angeles, the University of California-Los Angeles, Wheaton College (B.A., 1929), Westminster Theological Seminary (Th.B., 1932), University of Pennsylvania (M.A., 1932), and Bob Jones University (D.D., 1940). Drawn to youth ministry, the Saturday night rallies he launched in 1930 later developed into the Youth for Christ movement. Crawford was among the first evangelists in 1932 to appear on national radio with his *Young People's Church of the Air,* ultimately heard on some six hundred stations, including 450 outlets over the Mutual network. Crawford was the first gospel broadcaster in 1949 to purchase time on national network television. *Youth on the March* won a Sunday night audience in the millions, and Crawford was among the first to use an entertainment format rather than straight preaching. The program continued for two years, seen on a dozen stations coast to coast. Between 1958 and 1960, Crawford purchased six FM radio stations around the country, and Crawford Broadcasting remains a vital player in Christian radio today. In 1960 he became the first evangelical to purchase a television station. Though WPCA/Philadelphia frequently aired gospel programs, the station operated as a local network affiliate and was not licensed as an expressly religious outlet. During his life Crawford, who died in 1960, also founded Pinebrook Bible Conference in Stroudsburg, Pennsylvania, and The King's College (1938) in Briarcliff Manor, New York.

M. R. DeHaan and Richard DeHaan. Born in 1891 in Zeeland, Michigan, M. R. DeHaan was a successful physician when converted at age thirty-one and called to preach. After pastoring churches in Grand Rapids, Michigan, he was led of God into a new ministry. DeHaan, on the air since the 1920s, founded *Radio Bible Class* in 1938 on a single local station as an outgrowth of a weekly Bible study group, and served as its speaker until his death in 1965. By the 1940s he was heard on hundreds of stations, published the popular *Our Daily Bread,* and by the end of his career had authored twenty-five books. His son Richard assumed leadership of the ministry, having been trained for the task at Wheaton and Calvin colleges, with advanced study at Northern Baptist Seminary of Chicago. In his own right, Richard DeHaan has continued and built the nondenominational ministry into a worldwide outreach, and launched the top-rated *Day of Discovery* television program.

James Dobson. In 1977, with a Ph.D. from the University of Southern California (USC) in child development, Dobson had served fourteen years as associate clinical professor of pediatrics at the USC School of Medicine and a concurrent seventeen years on the attending staff of the Los Angeles Children's Hospital Division of Child Development and Medical Genetics. But that year, having seen firsthand the "massive internal and external pressures on American households," he decided to act. Starting with a two-room suite in Arcadia, California, Dobson launched a twenty-five-minute *Focus on the Family* weekly radio broadcast. By its fifteenth anniversary, the work had become a national movement, employing one thousand workers in more than fifty separate ministries from its new headquarters in Colorado Springs, Colorado. *Focus on the Family* is now heard daily on four thousand stations worldwide, joined by six other broadcasts, eight magazines, a book publishing arm, and perhaps the nation's leading Christian video production ministry.

Theodore Epp. Born in 1907 in Oraibi, Arizona, the son of missionaries to the Hopi Indians, Epp was led to the ministry soon after his conversion at age twenty. He attended the Bible Institute of Los Angeles and Hesston (Kansas) College, before graduating from Southwestern Baptist Theological Seminary in 1932 and pastoring a Mennonite church in Goltry, Oklahoma. There he met radio evangelist T. Myron Webb, whose *Back to the Bible* program originated in nearby Enid, and in 1936 he joined Webb full time. Two years later, while visiting his parents in Nebraska, Epp learned there was no daily gospel program in that state. Since Webb had changed the name of his program to *Bible Fellowship Hour*, Epp received permission to use the name *Back to the Bible* in founding his own radio ministry—first aired on May 1, 1939, over a 250-watt station in Lincoln, Nebraska. Later the broadcast was carried by more than six hundred stations. Epp published seventy books and two periodicals, *Good News Broadcaster* (later *Confident Living*) and *Young Ambassador* (later *Teen Quest*); established a correspondence school; and founded a Back to the Bible Missionary Agency (now International Ministries). Since his death in 1985, the Back to the Bible ministry has continued under directors Warren Wiersbe (1985–92) and Woodrow Kroll (1992–present).

Jerry Falwell. Born in 1933 in Lynchburg, Virginia, Falwell was converted to Christ in 1952. Along with his alcoholic father, young Falwell refused to attend church with his Christian mother. But when she left the house on Sundays, she turned up the radio so her son would wake up hearing the *Old-Fashioned Revival Hour* with Charles Fuller. After his conversion, Falwell gave up plans for an engineering degree and enrolled in Baptist Bible College of Springfield, Missouri. He was graduated in 1956 and returned home to Lynchburg, founding Thomas Road Baptist Church with thirty-five members in a defunct Donald Duck Bottling Company plant. From the start, Falwell also bought time on local radio and television. In 1970 his *Old Time Gospel Hour* (its name inspired by the old Fuller program) went into national television syndication. Within a few years, the broadcast appeared on more stations than any other syndicated program, religious or secular, in America. He frequently addressed moral and social issues, and in 1979 founded Moral Majority as a political education organization. In the 1980s, the group became a lightning rod both for Christian activism and liberal criticism. When the PTL scandal exploded in 1987, Falwell attempted to carry on the former media ministry of Jim Bakker but gave up the effort amid legal countermoves from Bakker loyalists. A month later he resigned as president of Moral Majority to rededicate his ministry to preaching the gospel. In 1989 Falwell disbanded Moral Majority, saying the group had served its purpose as a catalyst for Christian activism. Today the focus of his ministry is his church and Liberty University, a four-year liberal arts institution at Lynchburg that Falwell founded in 1971.

Paul Freed. Born in 1918, the son of missionaries, Freed spent his childhood in the Arab lands of the Middle East. He also entered the ministry, starting a church in Greensboro, North Carolina, and then becoming that city's local Youth for Christ (YFC) director. In 1948, however, Freed was challenged by YFC founder Torrey Johnson to consider the call of foreign missions, particularly Europe, in his own life. At an international YFC conference in Switzerland, he heard about the plight of Spanish believers under the Catholic traditionalist Franco regime. With God's leading, Freed founded the Voice of Tangier in 1954, a radio station able to reach Spain from across the Strait of Gibraltar. When Morocco gained independence in 1959 and nationalized all radio stations, Freed obtained an ultra-powerful site in Monte Carlo, Monaco, built by the Nazis during World War II and since abandoned. With an expanded vision for reaching all Europe, Freed established Trans World Radio (TWR) in 1960. He serves today with TWR, now headquartered in Cary, North Carolina, leading a global enterprise with eight radio transmitters that can be heard daily by 80 percent of the world's population in some one hundred languages.

Charles Fuller. Born in 1887 in southern California and raised in a Christian home, Fuller was graduated from Pomona College and entered the family orange growing business in 1910. He was converted to Christ at a 1916 Paul Rader revival meeting, then studied three years at the Bible Institute of Los Angeles. In 1920 he began an adult Bible class at a local mainline church but left over doctrinal differences. However, he kept the class together, and later it formed the nucleus of Calvary Church, which ordained and called Fuller as its pastor in 1925. At the same time, Fuller maintained a local radio ministry, which by the early 1930s had grown into a national outreach. His church did not share his vision for radio, so Fuller resigned in 1932 to establish an independent radio ministry. Ultimately, his two network programs drew an estimated national audience of twenty million listeners, and by 1943 his Good News Broadcasting Association purchased more airtime than any other broadcaster—religious or secular—in America. Fuller retired in 1967 and died two years later, but the *Old-Fashioned Revival Hour* broadcast (later renamed *The Joyful Sound*) continued until the early 1980s. Today the Fuller Theological Seminary, which the evangelist founded with Harold John Ockenga in 1947, still bears his name.

Billy Graham. Born in 1918 near Charlotte, North Carolina, Graham was converted at age sixteen during a revival meeting. He attended Bob Jones University (1936), Florida Bible Institute (1937–38), and Wheaton College (1940–43). After a brief pastorate in Illinois, Graham became staff evangelist (1944–47) of the newly formed Youth for Christ organization; then he was named president (1947–51) of Northwestern Bible College in Minneapolis, Minnesota. His experience with radio began in 1945, when he took over a local Chicago broadcast begun by YFC founder Torrey Johnson. Then in 1949, during his tenure at Northwestern, the school went on the air with station KTIS. That same year, a Graham crusade in Los Angeles vaulted him to national attention. During that event he committed himself to absolute belief in the authority of the Bible, which Graham later claimed was the turning point in his ministry. In 1950 he founded the Billy

Graham Evangelistic Association, and that year his *Hour of Decision* radio program and telecasts debuted. His growing reputation drew the attention of President Dwight Eisenhower, and from then on Graham became unofficial spiritual advisor to many U.S. presidents. However, his policy of organizing city crusades with the cooperation of non-evangelical churches attracted much comment. Criticism came to a head at the 1957 New York Crusade, the first crusade ever televised nationwide. After the event, many fundamentalists broke with Graham, saying "decision cards" signed by converts were sometimes given to liberal churches for follow-up. Nevertheless, he remains the most respected and admired evangelist in America, recognized as having preached the gospel to more people than any man in history. More than 100 million individuals have heard Graham in person, and two million have received Christ at his crusades. Millions more have been reached by radio, television, motion pictures, books, and periodicals.

E. Brandt Gustavson. Currently president of NRB, a post to which he was named in 1990, Gustavson formerly served as executive vice president of Trans World Radio (1986–90), vice president of Moody Bible Institute (1974–86), and director of the Moody Broadcasting Network (1967–74). Gustavson attended Northwestern College and Loyola University of Chicago, before beginning his career at Moody in 1961 as manager of its radio station in Cleveland. He also served with the Billy Graham association at KAIM/Honolulu.

David Hofer. Born in 1917 in Dinuba, California, Hofer was a student at the Bible Institute of Los Angeles when he felt called of God into the ministry of radio. While singing in a quartet with his brother Egon at a Youth for Christ rally in Dinuba, the two men heard about how local businessmen were praying for a gospel radio voice in California's vast Central Valley. The Hofers accepted the challenge and in 1946, ten years after David graduated from Biola, the brothers were licensed to operate KRDU from their hometown of Dinuba. The outlet was perhaps the first Christian station to be run as a commercial venture, profiting from the sale of advertising and of airtime to radio preachers. Hofer also owned Christian bookstores and was cofounder in 1955 of Hume Lake Christian Camps. He was NRB president from 1979 to 1982.

Rex Humbard. Born in 1919 in Little Rock, Arkansas, Humbard learned revivalism from an early age by traveling with the family's singing-and-crusade ministry led by his father. He met Maude Aimee, his wife, in 1942, and the couple traveled with the family team for ten years until establishing their own church ministry in Akron, Ohio. The church later became known as the Cathedral of Tomorrow, serving as a base for the television ministry Humbard began in 1953. In 1968 the Humbard program went into international syndication, with its pioneering variety entertainment format, and by the late 1970s the evangelist had amassed the largest independent station network in the world. His success inspired other preachers to enter the medium, ultimately driving up competition for Sunday time slots and viewer support. In 1985, Humbard was forced to cancel his program as revenues failed to keep pace with rising costs for airtime. While other broadcasters used highly visible construction projects to elicit viewer donations, Humbard had abandoned that approach in 1973 when plans for a Bible college and media center were denied by government intrusion. At the time he closed his television ministry, Humbard lamented that viewers would more readily give money for buildings than for evangelism.

Torrey Johnson. Though a prominent local broadcaster in Chicago during his early ministry, Johnson is better known today for his seminal influence on other men who became major figures in Christian broadcasting. After his graduation from Wheaton College and Northern Baptist Theological Seminary, in 1933 he was called to Midwest Bible Church, where he saw it become a leading evangelical congregation during twenty years of service.

In 1944 his church began sponsoring local youth rallies, a spontaneous national movement fostered by the ministry of broadcaster Percy Crawford, but which Johnson molded into a formalized Youth for Christ (YFC) organization in 1945. As YFC took more of his time, he persuaded a local pastor, Billy Graham, to take over his local *Songs in the Night* radio program. Later he also introduced Graham to the crusade ministry, bringing him on as YFC staff evangelist, a position from which Graham first gained a national reputation. It was Johnson who challenged Paul Freed to enter foreign missions, leading to the global ministry of Trans World Radio. And over the years, YFC exerted similar influences on many others. Johnson relinquished the YFC presidency in 1948 and left Midwest Bible Church in 1953, as the focus of his ministry turned to international crusade evangelism. From 1968 to 1983, he developed the Bibletown conference center in Boca Raton, Florida, and since then has continued as a popular Bible conference speaker.

Clarence Jones. Born in 1900 in Sherrard, Illinois, Jones was educated at Moody Bible Institute in Chicago. After graduation in 1921 as class president and valedictorian, he joined the staff of Paul Rader at Chicago Gospel Tabernacle. There he helped found the AWANA ("Approved Workmen Are Not Ashamed") youth program that today is a national organization. However, it was Rader's radio ministry that most influenced the young Jones. He played in the brass quartet that accompanied his mentor's first broadcast from the roof of Chicago City Hall, and helped as Rader went from a local program to a national network broadcast. In 1928 he toured South America to scout sites for a missionary radio station. A year later in Chicago he met Reuben Larson, an itinerant evangelist who had also gained a vision for missionary radio after hearing R. R. Brown at a church conference. The two men obtained a license from the government of Ecuador for a station near Quito—that nation's first broadcast facility and also the first missionary radio operation in the world. Station HCJB went on the air Christmas Day 1931. Today as World Radio Missionary Fellowship, the organization ministers around the world. Jones retired in 1961 and, until his death in 1986, traveled extensively to promote Christian missionary radio.

Marlin Maddoux. Starting in 1975 as a Dallas radio talk show, Maddoux's *Point of View* program gained a national daily audience in 1983 when it was picked up live by the Satellite Radio Network. Building on the success of the show, which is now produced by his International Christian Media ministry, Maddoux in 1985 established the USA Radio Network as "the first American news radio network to deal with key issues from the conservative standpoint." The network's news services are now carried by more than two hundred stations nationwide, and more than thirty radio news and talk personalities are featured each week. USA is also the first Christian radio network to be totally supported by advertising. Maddoux remains the host of *Point of View,* which now claims to be "the world's largest live radio ministry."

Walter Maier. Born in 1893 in Boston, Massachusetts, Maier was a scholar of the first order. He earned degrees from Boston College (1913), Concordia Seminary (1916), and Harvard University (M.A., 1920; Ph.D., 1929). Ordained by the Lutheran Church Missouri Synod (LCMS) in 1917, he was appointed head of the LCMS youth organization, the Walther League, three years later. In 1922 he left that post to become professor of Old Testament and Hebrew at Concordia Seminary in St. Louis. At his urging the school established radio station KFUO in 1924, with Maier as a regular speaker. Then in 1930, under the sponsorship of the LCMS Lutheran Laymen's League, he went on national radio with *The Lutheran Hour.* Ultimately the program became the largest radio venture of its time, aired on more than twelve hundred stations worldwide in thirty-six languages, with an estimated annual audience of nearly 700 million. Maier published more than twenty books, annually authored a daily devotional guide, and was editor of the Walther League magazine from 1922 to 1945. When he died in 1950, Maier had preached the gospel to more people than any man in history. *The Lutheran Hour* continues to this day under LCMS sponsorship.

J. Vernon McGee. Born in 1904 and raised in the South, McGee attended Columbia and Dallas Theological seminaries. After his ordination in 1933, he pastored Presbyterian churches in the South until called to the Church of the Open Door in Los Angeles—the church where broadcasters Charles Fuller and Percy Crawford had come to Christ years earlier. There he began *The Open Bible Hour* weekly radio program. In 1949, as an outgrowth of McGee's pulpit ministry, the show developed into a unique *Thru the Bible* daily broadcast. McGee taught the entire Bible consecutively, book by book and verse by verse, in a cycle of two and a half and, later, five years. He retired from the pastorate in 1970 and, by the end of the decade, *Thru the Bible* was heard worldwide on more than seven hundred stations in twelve languages. The ministry, headquartered in Pasadena, California, received more than one thousand letters per day from listeners. At the time of his death in 1988, McGee had taped more than twenty years of pre-recorded messages in the *Thru the Bible* cycle, so his ministry continues in a vital way to this day.

Aimee Semple McPherson. Born Aimee Kennedy in Ontario, Canada, she embraced Pentecostalism in 1908 and married the evangelist Robert Semple, who converted her. She was ordained a year later and, in 1910, departed for China as a missionary. Robert died three months after their arrival in China. In 1912 she married Harold McPherson, but left her husband in 1915 to become an itinerant evangelist. Later Harold rejoined her, as Aimee conducted widely publicized faith healing tent crusades from Maine to Florida. After the couple separated in 1918 (they were divorced in 1921) Aimee began a transcontinental tour that lasted five years, included some forty crusades, and crossed the country eight times. In 1922 she relinquished her Assemblies of God credentials and, claiming an inspiration, founded the "Church of the Foursquare Gospel" in 1923 by opening a five-thousand-seat church in Los Angeles. A year later, McPherson established radio station KFSG. She gained increasing notoriety in 1926 as an alleged victim of a kidnapping, in 1931 from her third marriage, and in 1935 from her subsequent divorce. McPherson died during 1944 in an Oakland hotel room from an accidental overdose. By then her movement had grown to six hundred churches and 22,000 members.

Paul Myers. Known for thirty-nine years as "First Mate Bob" of the Good Ship Grace, Myers began his *Haven of Rest* ministry in 1934 on a single Los Angeles station but soon built the broadcast into a national network broadcast. He had been a celebrated Hollywood movie and radio orchestra leader in the 1920s when alcohol brought him down. Myers left his family, soon descended into skid row and, one day in February 1934, found himself collapsed in a drunken stupor beside the San Diego harbor. He was awakened by the clanging of a ship's bell, stumbled into a seedy motel, and there found a Gideon Bible beside his bed. At once he accepted Christ and, thirty days later, was back on radio as First Mate Bob—taking a nautical theme inspired by his conversion experience. He remained as speaker until his death in 1973, and today *Haven of Rest* continues under the leadership of Ray Ortlund. Myers actively encouraged the ministries of his associates. Both Robert Bowman and Bob Pierce, founders respectively of the Far East Broadcasting Company and of World Vision, began their careers with Myers.

Paul Rader. Born in 1879 in Denver, Rader was the son of a Methodist pastor and revivalist. He attended secular universities until deciding to enter the ministry in 1906. After two churches in two years, moving from Massachusetts to Oregon, he became disillusioned and relocated to New York City. There Rader was impressed by a new evangelical movement, the Christian and Missionary Alliance (CMA), and began street preaching after a spiritual awakening in 1911. He reentered the ministry in 1912 as a CMA pastor in Pittsburgh until called in 1915 to the Moody Church in Chicago. Four years later, Rader was elected CMA president after the death of its founder and was in great demand as a crusade speaker. In 1922 he left Moody Church to found the Chicago Gospel Tabernacle and also began his radio ministry that year. By 1930 his *Breakfast Brigade* program was aired daily on CBS. Rader left the CMA movement in 1925 and founded Christian World Couriers, a missionary organization he headed until his death in 1938. He is author of two beloved hymns, "Only Believe" and "Old Time Power."

Oral Roberts. Born in 1918 in Pontotoc County, Oklahoma, Roberts rebelled against his upbringing as son of a Pentecostal minister, until he converted to Christ at age seventeen. A few days later, Roberts experienced what he believed was a divine healing from tuberculosis. He became an itinerant revivalist and was catapulted to national fame at a 1947 crusade when he narrowly missed death by an assassin's bullet. In 1954 he began a television ministry, but abandoned studio broadcasts the next year to become the first evangelist to produce programs directly from his tent services. Over the following years he built Oral Roberts University in Tulsa, Oklahoma (1960–65), played down his theological views and stopped holding crusades (1968), and took his television ministry into national syndication (1969) with a mainstream program that featured sophisticated production and prominent celebrity guests. In the 1970s, *Oral Roberts and You* was the highest rated religious program in the nation. However, Roberts became embroiled in several controversies during the 1980s. These actions tarnished his public reputation, but under his son Richard Roberts the television ministry and university continue to operate on a large scale.

Marion "Pat" Robertson. Born in 1930 in Lexington, Virginia, Robertson was born into one of the First Families of the Old

Dominion. He is descended from a signer of the Declaration of Independence and two U.S. presidents, and his father was a long-time U.S. senator from Virginia. Robertson was graduated from Washington and Lee University in 1950 and, after a brief Korean War tour as a Marine officer, entered Yale University Law School in 1952. After graduation in 1955, however, he failed the New York bar exam and went into business with a New York electronics firm. After his conversion in 1956, Robertson felt called to the ministry and enrolled at the Biblical Seminary of New York. He pastored in New York City for a time until, feeling compelled by God, he returned home to Virginia in 1959 and acquired a defunct UHF television station in Portsmouth. Robertson incorporated as the "Christian Broadcasting Network" with three dollars in the bank. In November 1960 he was licensed by the FCC to operate WYAH-TV as a primarily religious station, the first such station in America. Soon he added a radio station but by 1963, CBN was falling behind financially. A telethon that year, seeking seven hundred viewers to pledge ten dollars per month, kept the ministry afloat. In 1966 the annual *700 Club* telethon developed into a daily program, the first Christian talk show ever attempted. Since then, CBN has moved its headquarters to Virginia Beach and expanded almost continuously to the present day. Related ministries encompass The Family Channel cable network with nearly sixty million subscribers, two radio news networks, a motion picture company, a university, an international relief agency, a national political education movement, and a public service law center. Robertson first became interested in politics when he helped organize the Washington for Jesus rally in 1980, which drew nearly half a million participants. In 1986–88 he pursued the Republican nomination for president and, though defeated after limited early success, remains a force in the party today.

Charles Stanley. At the age of fourteen in Danville, Virginia, Stanley committed himself to pastoral ministry. From there he studied at the University of Richmond, Southwestern Baptist

Theological Seminary, and Luther Rice Seminary. Stanley pastored churches in North Carolina, Ohio, and Florida before his 1971 call to the First Baptist Church of Atlanta, now a congregation of twelve thousand members. He gained national attention as president of the Southern Baptist Convention (1984–86), winning election at a time when "conservative" and "moderate" factions were struggling for control of America's largest Protestant denomination. His *In Touch* program is aired daily on some five hundred radio stations, while a televised version is seen on more than one hundred outlets and several cable networks. Together the broadcasts reach a potential audience of eighty million households.

Lester Sumrall. Born in New Orleans, son of a devout Christian mother, Sumrall experienced in 1930 at age seventeen what he believed to be a divine healing from tuberculosis. Three weeks later he left his home in Florida to begin preaching. After two years of itinerant ministry, Sumrall was ordained and called to pastor an Arkansas church. In 1934 he resigned the church and, feeling led to a ministry of missionary evangelism, took ship in San Francisco bound for Tahiti. Ultimately he started a church in Australia, then left that country to travel and preach throughout Asia and Eastern Europe, and later throughout Central and South America. Sumrall returned to pastoral ministry in 1947 when he founded the South Bend, Indiana, Gospel Tabernacle. But after taking leaves of absence to minister in the Philippines (1952–54) and Israel (1956–57), he resigned in 1959 to begin a new church in Hong Kong. Four years later Sumrall returned to South Bend and, in 1968, began radio and television broadcasting over local stations his ministry acquired. Today, LeSea (Lester Sumrall Evangelistic Association) Broadcasting is a key player in Christian radio and television.

Charles Swindoll. Born in 1934 in El Campo, Texas, Swindoll was a U.S. Marine when God called him to pastoral ministry. He entered Dallas Theological Seminary in 1959 and, after graduation in 1963, served churches in Massachusetts and Texas. However, his reputation as an expository preacher, author, and broadcaster was established at First Evangelical Free Church of Fullerton, California, where Swindoll became senior pastor in 1971. His *Insight for Living* ministry encompasses cassette tape distribution and a thirty-minute radio broadcast aired more than sixteen hundred times daily on stations nationwide. At present, Swindoll's published works include more than two dozen books and a comparable number of booklets. In 1993 he was named president of Dallas Theological Seminary.

Abe Van Der Puy. Born in 1919 in Sheboygan, Wisconsin, Van Der Puy trusted Christ as a high school senior and enrolled at Wheaton College, graduating in 1941. After studying at Calvin Seminary, he became a missionary in Ecuador with HCJB World Radio, often operating the Gospel Sound Truck for outdoor evangelistic meetings. Over the years Van Der Puy was named by the mission as HCJB radio station manager (1950), Ecuador field director (1955), and ultimately international president (1962). During twenty years in the post, his leadership helped build World Radio Missionary Fellowship into a worldwide outreach. Today he serves the organization, whose headquarters are now in Colorado Springs, Colorado, as chairman of the board. Beginning in 1979, Van Der Puy was heard on the *Voice of Missions* weekly broadcast sponsored by the Back to the Bible ministry.

Appendix C

RELIGIOUS BROADCASTING HALL OF FAME, NRB FOUNDERS, AND NRB CHAIRMEN

HALL OF FAME

Presented to a living or deceased individual who, for a significant period of time, has made an outstanding contribution in the field of Christian broadcasting with the highest of standards and faithfulness to Christ, and of whom it can be testified, "I have fought a good fight, I have finished my course, I have kept the faith" (2 Tim. 4:7).

William Ward Ayer (1892–1985)
Inducted 1978
NRB Founding President
New York, New York

Donald Grey Barnhouse (1896–1960)
Inducted 1978
Bible Study Hour
Philadelphia, Pennsylvania

Eugene Bertermann (1914–83)
Inducted 1984
Lutheran Laymen's League
St. Louis, Missouri

Myron Boyd (1908–78)
Inducted 1980
Light and Life Hour
Seattle, Washington

R. R. Brown (1885–1964)
Inducted 1976
World Radio Congregation
Omaha, Nebraska

Lois Crawford (1892–1986)
Inducted 1977
KFGQ Radio
Boone, Iowa

Percy Crawford (1902–60)
Inducted 1982
Youth on the March
Briarcliff Manor, New York

Richard DeHaan
Inducted 1983
Radio Bible Class
Grand Rapids, Michigan

James Dobson
Inducted 1991
Focus on the Family
Colorado Springs, Colorado

Bruce Dunn (1919–93)
Inducted 1994
Grace Worship Hour
Peoria, Illinois

Theodore Epp (1907–85)
Inducted 1986
Back to the Bible
Lincoln, Nebraska

Jerry Falwell
Inducted 1985
Old Time Gospel Hour
Lynchburg, Virginia

Charles Fuller (1887–1969)
Inducted 1975
Old-Fashioned Revival Hour
Pasadena, California

Herman Gockel
Inducted 1979
This Is the Life
St. Louis, Missouri

Billy Graham
Inducted 1981
Hour of Decision
Minneapolis, Minnesota

Rex Humbard
Inducted 1991
Rex Humbard Ministry
Boca Raton, Florida

Clarence Jones (1900–1986)
Inducted 1975
HCJB World Radio
Quito, Ecuador

M. G. (Pat) Robertson
Inducted 1986
CBN/The Family Channel
Virginia Beach, Virginia

Walter Maier (1893–1950)
Inducted 1975
The Lutheran Hour
St. Louis, Missouri

Lester Roloff (1914–82)
Inducted 1993
The Family Altar
Corpus Christi, Texas

J. Vernon McGee (1904–88)
Inducted 1989
Thru the Bible
Pasadena, California

Carl Smith
Inducted 1994
Consulting Radio Engineer
Brecksville, Ohio

Paul Myers (1896–1973)
Inducted 1977
Haven of Rest
Los Angeles, California

Charles Stanley
Inducted 1988
In Touch Ministry
Atlanta, Georgia

George Palmer (1895–1981)
Inducted 1976
Morning Cheer
North East, Maryland

C. M. Ward
Inducted 1993
Revivaltime
Springfield, Missouri

Bill Pearce
Inducted 1992
Nightsounds
Rockford, Illinois

Thomas Zimmerman (1912–91)
Inducted 1987
Assemblies of God
Springfield, Missouri

Paul Rader (1879–1938)
Inducted 1976
The Breakfast Brigade
Chicago, Illinois

John Zoller (1888–1979)
Inducted 1975
Christ for Everyone
Detroit, Michigan

NRB FOUNDERS

National Religious Broadcasters was founded April 12, 1944, in Columbus, Ohio, and ratified by constitutional convention on

September 21, 1944, in Chicago, Illinois. The association was incorporated on December 18, 1944.

William Ward Ayer (1892–1985)
Calvary Baptist Church
New York, New York

Myron Boyd (1908–78)
Light and Life Hour
Seattle, Washington

Dale Crowley, Sr.
Right Start for the Day
Washington, D.C.

Howard Ferrin (1889–1993)
President, Barrington College
Barrington, Rhode Island

Torrey Johnson
Founder, Youth for Christ
Wheaton, Illinois

Bob Jones, Sr. (1883–1968)
Founder, Bob Jones University
Greenville, South Carolina

Charles Leaming (1905–88)
Faith Gospel Broadcast
St. Petersburg, Florida

Paul Myers (1896–1973)
Haven of Rest
Los Angeles, California

James Murch (1886–1973)
The Christians' Hour
Cincinnati, Ohio

Glenn Tingley (1901–88)
Radio Revival Hour
Toccoa Falls, Georgia

Thomas Zimmerman (1912–91)
Assemblies of God
Springfield, Missouri

John Zoller (1888–1979)
Christ for Everyone
Detroit, Michigan

NRB CHAIRMEN

Chairmen are listed by ministry affiliation at their time of NRB service.

1944–45 William Ward Ayer
Calvary Baptist Church
New York, New York

1945–47 Clinton Churchill
WKBW-AM Radio
Buffalo, New York

1948–52 Theodore Elsner
Gospel Tabernacle
Philadelphia, Pennsylvania

1952–53 Myron Boyd
Light and Life Hour
Seattle, Washington

1954–56 Thomas Zimmerman
Assemblies of God
Springfield, Missouri

1956–57 James Murch
The Christians' Hour
Cincinnati, Ohio

1957–75 Eugene Bertermann
Lutheran Laymen's League
St. Louis, Missouri

1975–78 Abe Van Der Puy
World Radio Missionary Fellowship
Colorado Springs, Colorado

1979–82 David Hofer
KRDU-AM Radio
Dinuba, California

1982–85 E. Brandt Gustavson
Moody Broadcasting Network
Chicago, Illinois

1985–88 Robert Cook
The King's Hour
Briarcliff Manor, New York

1988–91 Jerry Rose
WCFC-TV Channel 38
Chicago, Illinois

1991–94 David Clark
KMC Media
Dallas, Texas

1994 Robert Straton
Walter Bennett Communications
Philadelphia, Pennsylvania

BIBLIOGRAPHY

Armstrong, Ben. *The Electric Church*. Nashville, Tenn.: Thomas Nelson, 1979.

———. *The Fourth Network*. Unpublished manuscript. Parsippany, N.J.: National Religious Broadcasters, c. 1986.

Blewett, Lois, and Bob Blewett. *Twenty Years under God*. Minneapolis: World Wide Publications, 1970.

Bloom, Naomi, ed. *Giving the Winds a Mighty Voice*. St. Paul: Northwestern College Radio Network, 1979.

Crawford, Lois. *When God and Papa Ganged Up Against Me*. Boone, Iowa: Boone Biblical College, 1977.

Crouch, Paul. *Ten Years of God's Miracles*. Santa Ana: Trinity Broadcasting Network, 1983.

Frankl, Razelle. *Televangelism: The Marketing of Popular Religion*. Carbondale, Ill.: Southern Illinois University Press, 1987.

Freed, Paul. *Trans World Radio: Towers to Eternity*. Nashville: Thomas Nelson, 1979.

Haddon, Jeffrey, and Anson Shuppe. *Televangelism: Power and Politics on God's Frontier*. New York: Henry Holt and Co., 1988.

Hill, George. *Airwaves to the Soul*. Saratoga, Calif.: R and E Publishers, 1983.

Hilliard, Robert, ed. *Radio Broadcasting*, 2d ed. New York: Hastings House, 1979.

———. *Television Broadcasting*. New York: Hastings House, 1979.

Humbard, Rex. *The Humbard Heritage*. Akron, Ohio: The Rex Humbard Ministry, 1977.

Ledyard, Gleason. *Skywaves: The Incredible Far East Broadcasting Company Story*. Chicago: Moody Press, 1968.

Lloyd, Mark. *Pioneers of Prime Time Religion*. Dubuque, Iowa: Kendall Hunt, 1988.

Matthews, Arthur. *Standing Up, Standing Together*. Carol Stream, Ill.: National Association of Evangelicals, 1992.

Murch, James DeForest. *Adventuring for Christ in Changing Times*. Louisville: Restoration Press, 1973.

Powell, Bill, et al. "Eyes on the Future." In *Newsweek*. May 31, 1993.

Reid, Daniel, et al., eds. *Dictionary of Christianity in America*. Downers Grove, Ill.: InterVarsity Press, 1990.

Siedell, Barry. *Gospel Radio*. Lincoln: The Good News Broadcasting Association, 1971.

"What God Hath Wrought." In *Religious Broadcasting*. February 1983.

INDEX